THE BOTTOM LINE HR FUNCTION

CHANDOS BUSINESS GUIDES
HUMAN RESOURCES & TRAINING

Chandos Business Guides are designed to provide managers with practical, down-to-earth information. The Chandos Business Guides are written by leading authors in their respective fields. If you would like to receive a full listing of current and forthcoming titles, please visit our web site www.chandospublishing.com or contact Melinda Taylor on email mtaylor@chandospublishing.com or telephone number +44 (0) 1865 882727.

New authors: we are always pleased to receive ideas for new titles; if you would like to write a Chandos Business Guide, please contact Dr Glyn Jones on email gjones@chandospublishing.com or direct telephone number +44 (0) 1865 884447.

THE BOTTOM LINE HR FUNCTION

PAUL KEARNS

Chandos Publishing

Oxford · England

Chandos Publishing (Oxford) Limited
Chandos House
5 & 6 Steadys Lane
Stanton Harcourt
Oxford OX8 1RL
England
Tel: +44 (0) 1865 882727 Fax: +44 (0) 1865 884448
Email: sales@chandospublishing.com
www.chandospublishing.com

••

First published in Great Britain in 2001

ISBN 1 902375 62 9

Typeset by Boyd Elliott Typesetting
Printed in England

To Nuala, Clare, Emily and Daniel

If you ever wondered what I have been doing for the past ten years then this is the best explanation I can give.

Contents

You are either going to love this or hate it …

In 1991 I set up a network for HR people who were interested in making a significant impact on their organisation's bottom line. It was very difficult getting any HR people interested. I called it PHIRM (pronounced 'firm') and yes I know it's an awful pun but it stood for Profitable Human Investment and Resource Management. As a result of running this network I was asked to speak at a whole range of events. Here is a letter of thanks I received after doing a talk to a joint branch meeting of the UK's Institutes of Management and Personnel Management (now the IPD).

From: The Chair of the Institute of Management

13 December 1993

Dear Paul

Regrettably, being a PHIRM believer has not made me any more of a PROMPT writer of thank you letters. Please, however accept my belated but sincere thanks for your talk to the joint IM and IPM meeting on 16 November.

While I appreciated that your approach was likely to be controversial with the IPM, I was surprised to discover the extent to which my colleagues on the IM committee had been stimulated. Their responses ranged from 'I can't see it myself' to 'It completely changed the nature of a meeting I held the next day'. I have to say it was one of the most lively sessions I can remember and personally I have taken much of your approach to heart. We are compiling nationally a list of speakers; would you mind being included on it?

I hope you are successful in progressing your more business-like approach to HR management because I feel British industry badly needs it and I look forward to watching the advancement of your career in the next decade.

With seasonal best wishes

Yours sincerely

Chair, IM

I was a bit worried at the time about her reference to 'the advancement of your career in the next decade'. Would it really take that long?

Seven years into the 'next decade', here is the story so far.

Choose your own introduction

The bottom line HR function doesn't exist – yet. Some organisations are working towards having an HR function that is totally focused on contributing to bottom line performance. However, all the HR functions I know of still have a long way to go. Whether you believe you have a bottom line HR function or not, by the time you have read this book you may have a different view of what is required to deserve that title.

Depending on your own job title and position you might like to start here by choosing your own introduction.

Director

You get the HR function you deserve.

You may currently regard working with personnel and training people in the same way that actors view having to work with children and animals. Alternatively, you may genuinely believe that your HR function really does make a great contribution to your business. Whatever your present perception is, this book is going to challenge that perception and offer other options.

From a practical perspective, this book contains some principles and tools that you can start to apply to your HR function immediately.

One of these tools is designed to help you gauge the real value contributed by HR.

The section that you should be particularly interested in, though, is Chapter 7 on HR strategy. By the end of this book I am hoping that you will agree that HR is of limited use if there is no HR strategy in place.

Operational/line manager

Your perception of HR may be that they are only there for when you need them, for example to help with recruitment or to offer advice on a disciplinary matter. Perhaps the training department are seen as the 'people who run courses' for your staff. You may feel that the service you receive is fantastic or, conversely, you might believe HR always makes a real meal out of everything they touch.

This book is very critical of many of the things HR functions do and tries to encourage them to provide a much better service to people like you. However, it takes two to tango and this book recommends a relationship between line managers and HR people which is much more like that of a partnership than a master/servant relationship.

If you want to get the best out of HR this book will suggest that you may have to fundamentally change your own thinking. All any author can ask is that you keep an open mind, at least until you finish the book.

HR director/manager

First, my apologies. This book is not meant to be a comfortable read for HR people. I have worked in this game for over twenty years and have always had doubts about the path followed by most HR functions. My work over the last ten years has done nothing to cause me to moderate those views. In fact, I am more convinced now than ever that HR functions have to fundamentally reinvent themselves if they are to make a significant, added value contribution.

If this book is highly critical it is meant to be constructively so. Virtually every organisation I have come into contact with could get significantly more value out of its human resource. Furthermore, I think the right sort of HR function should be the authors and architects of maximising organisational performance through people.

I hope you stick with the book throughout and, as I often say to my conference audiences, the only thing I cannot abide is indifference. I would rather this book generated a strong, adverse reaction from you than total indifference. At least that would mean you had read the book and thought about it. I'll keep my fingers crossed, though, in the hope that you will actually benefit from it.

But before you start, a short and simple exercise

Have a quick look at this exercise. It is designed to make you think about your own views and perceptions of the world of Human Resource Management.

First, do you believe there is a distinction to be made between soft organisational issues and hard business measures? So, for example, is employee counselling something you regard as soft? As compared to increasing production per hour, which could be considered to produce hard results. If you do not know what I mean then look at the list of headings below and start to categorise them as either 'soft', 'hard' or 'don't know'.

Making a profit   Reducing costs

Listening   Changing the culture

Motivating	Involving staff
Counselling	Selling
Improving quality	Motivating
Raising morale	Raising prices
Coaching	Developing staff
Empowering	Changing attitudes

Regardless of how you score these two lists of headings, are they not all supposed to produce hard results? Selling and making a profit obviously produce hard, measurable results. But do the other activities not also produce hard results? You counsel employees to help them deal with their problems – problems that make them inefficient, ineffective or unable to come to work. Either way, if the counselling helps them then there will be an improvement in something hard such as absentee rates, an improvement in efficiency or a more effective job completed because they are able to concentrate on their work more.

The reason for asking these questions is that many HR functions are given the task of looking after the so-called 'soft', people issues when, in fact, their work should focus on hard business measures as much any other function.

The bottom line HR function makes no distinction between soft and hard.

Terminology – how important is it in HR?

The term 'HRM' in this book can mean the subject, the function, the field of study or a body of knowledge, but often it gets shortened to just HR.

I use the term 'personnel' or 'personnel management' when I want to refer to the purely administrative and transactional role of the function.

As with any subject, terminology can be very important but in HR it is particularly so. How organisations manage their people is tied up with values, morals and even philosophy. These can very often result in highly emotive language. I have been described as being 'very hard-nosed' (not a description normally associated with HR professionals). I know what they mean but it is actually a very emotive term. A macho manager might take it as a compliment but it is rarely intended to be one. I think a better description of my approach is 'very business focused'. This may mean taking some very tough, difficult decisions but it is not the same as being hard-nosed.

Trying to use accurate, unemotional language in HR is very important. Even more important is making sure everyone concerned has the same, or at least a similar, understanding of the words being used.

I often describe some HR people as 'touchy feely'. One client once described his management development colleagues to me as 'luvvies'. As far as I am concerned both of these terms are used pejoratively but some HR people pride themselves on what they believe to be their strengths in people skills and their sensitivity to others.

Without wanting to pre-empt anything to be covered later in the book I will do my best to avoid using such language. As we will see very soon, effective management of the softer HR issues can indeed reap great rewards. On the other hand woolly thinking and a lack of clear objectives can often produce wasted activity.

About the author

Paul Kearns is widely recognised as a leading authority in the field of performance measurement and evaluation and has a reputation as a business-focused, human resource management professional. He founded the Personnel Works Partnership in 1990 specialising in improving individual and organisational performance through business linked HR strategies.

A popular and thought-provoking conference speaker on the subjects of HR strategy, measurement and evaluation he is an outspoken critic of modern management fads and fashions, preferring pragmatic solutions to complex business problems. He firmly believes that all business issues can be addressed in a simple, 'down-to-earth' way but he has found this approach to be so rare that he now refers to it as 'leading edge common sense'!

Paul Kearns is the author of several books:

* *Measuring HR and the Impact on the Bottom Line* (1995)

* *Measuring the Impact of Training and Development on the Bottom Line* (1996)

* *Measuring and Managing Employee Performance* (2000)

* *Maximise Your ROI in Training* (2000)

All of these titles are published by Financial Times/Prentice Hall.

Paul can be contacted at:

Personnel Works
PO Box 109
Henleaze
Bristol BS9 4DH
UK

Phone   +44 (0) 117 914 6984
Fax   +44 (0) 117 914 6978
Email   pkearns@breathemail.net

PART 1

Do you need a new HR function?

CHAPTER 1

What's wrong with personnel?

Would it be too harsh to sum up the current state of the average personnel function as the wrong function, performing the wrong role, employing the wrong people, doing the wrong things with the wrong systems, tools and processes? Possibly, but it is fair to say that the HR function has managed to earn itself an awful reputation.

Now, before you decide to ask for a refund, I am not the only person who seems to have come to this conclusion. Dave Ulrich, probably the most highly respected, award-winning academic working in the HR field in America, seems to hold similar views. So I presume he knows what he's talking about when he says:

> As much as I like HR people – I have been working in the field as a researcher, professor, and consultant for 20 years – I must agree that there is good reason for HR's beleaguered reputation. It is often ineffective, incompetent, and costly; in a phrase, it is value sapping. Indeed, if HR were to remain configured as it is today in many companies, I would have to answer the question above with a resounding 'Yes – abolish the thing'.[1]

Personnel's awful reputation

In December 1999 I spoke to a group of about 50 personnel staff in a very large computer systems company, a UK household name with a good pedigree. I was there at the invitation of the personnel director to inject some new thinking into his team. I started my talk by asking the question: 'How many of you believe you do a really good job?' Not one hand was raised.

I was genuinely surprised, although I have had similar responses to this question in the past. Anyway, I laughed and told them that this was an easy question to answer, we would come to the difficult ones later. So I asked them the same question again, while suggesting to them that the only answer to this question should be an unequivocal 'yes', regardless of whether they believed it or not and especially as their boss was in the audience. A few embarrassed titters could then be heard as one or two of them gradually, hesitantly but obediently raised their hands. I was making them all feel very uncomfortable.

The sadistic side of my nature then kicked in with 'OK, so you all do a good job [*sic*] but how many of you think that you really add value?' Well, considering the non-existent response to the first question this was now purely rhetorical. I think some of the audience would have described it as metaphysical if they knew what the word meant.

No, I am being extremely rude and patronising. These people are not stupid. By any conventional measure this group were highly intelligent. Many of them would be graduates and, as they worked for this particular company, they would be pretty good graduates. So why this incredible reaction to the simplest of questions? The answer is mindset, not intelligence.

Personnel professionals have a truly obscure mindset that has been fashioned and shaped out of a failure to ever get to grips with the simplest, most basic questions about their role. They operate on a highly intuitive level. In their bones they feel they are doing the right things but they have never bothered to try and produce evidence to support their intuition.

So, are they doing the right things? A research project by Roffey Park Management School in the UK showed that over 60 per cent of firms studied think:

> HR is too reactive. Most say that the department spends too much time on trivial matters. (*Personnel Today*, 14 December 1999)

In another study by Cranfield School of Management (reported in *Personnel Today*, 18 January 2000) only half of HR Directors surveyed had a seat on their board and a higher percentage admitted that they were not consulted on corporate strategy.

Earlier in 1999 it was also reported that SOCPO (the Society of Chief Personnel Officers in UK local government) was left off the government's consultation list for its 'Best Value' plans, a key plank in its public sector modernisation initiative.

This paints a very gloomy picture of personnel in the UK, so what about our American cousins? How about this from Thomas A. Stewart, a well-respected American business writer. In *Fortune* magazine on 15 January 1996, under the title 'Taking on the last bureaucracy', he criticised HR because:

> Nearly every function of this department can be performed more expertly, for less, by others. Chances are its leaders are unable to describe their contribution to value added except in trendy, unquantifiable and wannabe terms. Why not blow the sucker up?

There is plenty of evidence that personnel has a serious image problem. As a result, personnel and HR departments are under increasing pressure, not only to justify their existence, but also to offer greater value to their organisations and to demonstrate their contribution.

Therein lies the problem. From the HR practitioners' standpoint, those who have lost their jobs to outsourcers or have been transferred to an HR service centre have failed to convince their masters that HR work is anything more than a cost or necessary evil.

Many managing directors and finance directors believe that HR work is just a commodity that can be put out to the lowest bidder. If the HR function is just involved in transactional, day-to-day operational and administrative personnel tasks then why not outsource it and gain from efficiency savings?

Against this backdrop, there has been a continuing evolution of the role of the personnel function away from the traditional one of welfare and administration and more towards that of a strategic, business partner.

Whatever the conventional HR function has been doing, there is still the question: 'Could we have an HR function that adds a great deal more value?' This is not just a case of looking at cost or efficiency, although they will always form part of the equation, but involves considering whether HR has a much more fundamental role to play in improving individual and organisational performance, in a way that no other function can.

This book gets to grips with all of these issues and offers guidance to directors and managers on how to reposition their HR function. It also gives HRM practitioners a clearly defined role as a business partner with some of the skills, tools and techniques necessary to fulfil this role.

But first, the oldest terminological debate in the field of people management. Do we call it personnel or HR?

The HR versus personnel debate

One debate that has been raging inside the profession for many years is the question of whether to use the term Human Resource Management or Personnel Management. On one level this is just a matter of personal preference or mere semantics and you would not expect it to still be causing a fuss. Yet as recently as 8 February 2000 these words from Mike Judge, Personnel Director of Peugeot, were written in *Personnel Today*:

> The trend in the past few years to call ourselves the 'human resources department' sends out signals about ourselves and our profession that I hope are not true . . . Frankly I find the term 'human resource' to be demeaning to working people. The term sends all the wrong messages and I cannot believe employees in whichever enterprise are happy to regard themselves as 'resources'.

I have never met Mike Judge but he sounds very passionate in his defence of personnel as a title. In the final analysis, it should not matter too much what title is used, but it does. It matters because words have connotations and long-standing perceptions and misconceptions. It also matters because if we do not regard people as organisational resources then we are being dishonest to the organisation and to the employees. Anyone who has been made redundant knows exactly what it feels like to be treated as a dispensable resource. But then so do the highest earners as well.

Resource is the best word I can think of to describe employees. Those who want to regard people as 'personnel' are probably unlikely to develop effective, business-focused HR strategies. How can they when they are afraid to admit that people are, essentially, a potentially very valuable but, equally, expendable resource?

This book starts from the premise that HRM is a very different entity to personnel management and it will try to make some clear distinctions between the two. I never used to mind too much whether I was called an HR manager or a personnel manager, now I mind very much. HRM, when it is being done well, is a world away from personnel management.

This debate will continue, no doubt, but it is a distraction and it gets in the way of organisations learning how to manage their people better. What is particularly worrying, though, especially from the profession's viewpoint, is that this debate still rages on in the minds of those who should be leading.

Look at these quotes from Geoff Armstrong who has been the Director-General of the UK's Institute of Personnel and Development (IPD) since 1992. They are taken from his review, published in *People Management* (23 February 1995), of a book entitled *Human Resource Management: A Critical Text*.[2]

> The HRM rhetoric doesn't survive the business reality ... Managers see their overriding priorities as being to cut costs, focus on core activities, outsource everything else, and satisfy the expectations of investing institutions above other stakeholders. And the drive for continuous improvement usually means fewer jobs. So the HRM ideals – empowerment, involvement, personal growth – are bound to be frustrated.

It seems that Armstrong does not like the whole idea of HRM very much, but that is beside the point. If we try to read between the lines we could be forgiven for coming to some unexpected conclusions.

First, does HRM actually subscribe to a set of ideals as Armstrong implies? I regard myself as an HR professional and I do not have any fixed ideals. In my version of HRM it makes absolute business sense for

McDonald's to live with a very high level of staff turnover and to not worry too much about empowering their employees. I can also see that in a casualty department at a hospital maybe empowerment is the name of the game if immediate, life-saving action is required. HRM is about having the right human resource policies for the circumstances that the business faces. It does not assume empowerment is a good thing.

If we can stick with the notion of empowerment for a second, the only reason for empowering employees, as far as HR is concerned, is that it can make very good business sense – as long as it is implemented carefully. I also happen to believe that empowered employees are generally more satisfied employees. This is where we move into the area of 'ideals'. I have to admit that I do prefer the idea of employees becoming more involved and more empowered. It can make their working lives much more rewarding and I will happily subscribe to that but only on the basis that it can be a win/win situation. The effect on employees is the beneficial by-product, the icing on the cake. The *raison d'être* for pursuing empowerment policies should always be that they are in the best interests of the organisation. Now, does that sound hard-nosed or touchy feely? That particular question now appears to be an irrelevance.

A second, more alarming, point about Armstrong's views is that he appears to be suggesting that organisations cannot have the best of both worlds. They cannot, for example, attempt to drive down costs and simultaneously encourage the involvement of their employees. Yet the evidence is clear and obvious that those organisations, which need to drive down costs continuously, have to involve employees as much as possible in this process if they are to achieve long-term cost reductions. In other words, effective HRM and high performing organisations become mutually inclusive, not mutually exclusive. It is the one-dimensional thinking of downsizing that tries to cut costs without employing effective HR strategies, and we have all seen some of the disastrous results of short-termist downsizing initiatives.

The final and most depressing point, for IPD members and students, is that Armstrong, as Director-General of the IPD, surely has some responsibility for leading and directing the profession at large. If he writes off HRM, one can only assume that he accepts a much less strategic role for personnel, a role that is much closer to the traditional role of the welfare and administration function. He finishes his review with the comment:

> In my view … it is wrong to tie strategic people issues to the HRM bandwagon. They were around before HRM was invented, and will still be around a long time after its faddish label has faded.

I am not sure whether Armstrong believes that some personnel specialists are already operating strategically or not. Certainly, just changing the function's name to HRM does not guarantee anything. So it might be helpful to try and clear up some common misunderstandings and misconceptions about HRM, about what it can contribute and the relative value of personnel activity as opposed to HRM activity.

The starting point for this discussion will be the construction of a model of HRM.

HR models, paradigms and the 'conventional wisdom'

The conventional wisdom in personnel circles, like many other professions, is that there is a body of knowledge and good practice which can be applied, more or less regardless of the organisational environment and circumstances in which you have to work. This thinking could be described as working to a particular paradigm. The paradigm for accountants, for example, is all about direct and indirect costs and ultimately balancing the books (we will look at this particular paradigm in more detail later).

Take a new personnel manager who operates in accordance with their professional training; they would work to a particular pattern. Each job would have to have a job description and pay would be determined by a structured pay and grading system, usually based on the use of job evaluation techniques. Each employee would be appraised on a regular basis both in terms of their performance and their ongoing training and development needs. The aggregated training needs identified at these discussions would then form the basis of a company training plan.

This paradigm is very simplistic and rather rigid. It evolved during a period when any professionalism was probably better than none. Stronger unionisation also played its part, so part of the paradigm is the need to treat all employees fairly and consistently (hence the use of job evaluation to produce a felt-fair pay system). However, it generally only fitted well in organisations that were not going through much change. So structured career paths were possible with development plans to match.

There was never a 'golden era' of HRM but the realities of organisational life have certainly shifted significantly since then. But has there been a corresponding shift in the personnel management paradigm? First we need to look at a normal model of personnel management to see how it might need to change.

A simple model of personnel management

The model illustrated in Figure 1.1 is a very simple, almost two-dimensional, model of how an organisation tries to manage its people.

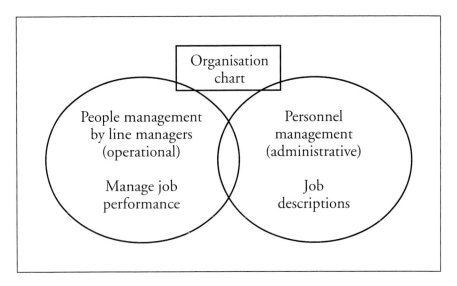

Figure 1.1 A simple model of personnel management.

Imagine that you are a managing director (MD) starting up a new company. The first conscious decision you will have to make regarding people will be an organisation chart, even if this is rather fluid in the early days and not particularly explicit. So the first employee is someone given the title of sales manager. The second employee is a personnel manager to handle a heavy recruitment workload.

Once the organisation chart is in place your personnel manager drafts some job descriptions based on the organisation chart. So job descriptions for the sales manager and a group of sales representatives are prepared. These are then used by the personnel manager to help the sales manager decide on the sort of people you need to attract, their skills and experience and the rewards you will have to offer them. The 'personnel' element of this work is important but it is, by and large, of an administrative nature and shown by the circle on the right.

The role of the personnel manager might end at the stage where the new salespeople have joined the company and signed their employment contracts. How they actually perform in the job is then the responsibility of the new sales manager and is shown by the circle on the left. However, on odd occasions, when the sales manager wants to make any changes to the reward system or perhaps fire an underperformer, they may well seek the advice and support of the personnel manager. This is represented in the diagram by an area of overlap between the roles of the personnel manager and the sales manager.

This is probably the simplest model of where personnel management fits and is a reasonable reflection of the relationship between the line and personnel. On a day-to-day basis, how much involvement the personnel manager has in the management of the sales team will be dictated, to a great extent, by the relationship between the two managers. However, the buck stops with the sales manager who is ultimately responsible for sales performance.

Personnel's traditional role

In this simple company the role of the personnel manager (and the function) can be characterised by the following elements:

- The personnel manager is totally *reactive*. They have been handed an organisation chart and then had to recruit against that. They have no say in how the organisation chart was designed or whether the budget for recruitment and salaries will be enough to recruit the necessary quality of staff for the business to run smoothly.

- Personnel is an additional cost to the business and is likely to be shown in the accounts as an *overhead*. Both the MD and/or the sales manager could do some of the personnel manager's work but the cost of personnel is viewed as necessary.

- The personnel manager is *not directly accountable* for the performance of the sales team, especially as the final recruitment decision is always down to the sales manager.

- The personnel manager uses *standard techniques* for writing job descriptions and person specifications.

- There are *no measures* in place for how the personnel manager is performing.

- Because the personnel manager is not held accountable for sales performance he believes there is *no real element of risk* in his role.

- If you, as the MD, felt at a later stage that you had to change the organisation structure the personnel manager would take the new chart and try to ensure that any recruitment or redundancy work is handled correctly. But the personnel manager would not see it as part of his or her role to suggest any structural changes until you raised the subject. This is a *very static model* of personnel management

It is true to say that many personnel people still see this as a reasonable description of their role. If they are very good at their job then they can provide a very effective support service. They may even be very efficient in recruiting new staff, enough to make employing an outside agency unnecessary. If this is the model that the company is happy to work to then there should be no serious disagreements about personnel's role, as long as the tasks continue to be performed well.

I have consciously described this role, though, in a way which requires a minimal amount of 'involvement' by the personnel manager in the running of the business. In this role they are doing everything very professionally but their impact on the business is minimal. For any organisation needing to fundamentally change, to meet the changing needs of the market, this role is no longer enough.

Two mental models for HRM

> My job early on was to make people happy ... But when we viewed our role in HR as keeping people happy, we found ourselves on a separate track from operating managers who were concerned with such things as yield, billing, scrap and other hard business issues. (Chuck Neilson, VP-HR, Texas Instruments, in *Personnel Journal*, August 1994)

This quote from Chuck Neilson, who has worked in HR for well over 20 years, is very illuminating for two reasons. He obviously works to a model, or paradigm, of what personnel or HRM should be. More importantly, regardless of the paradigm that he used to work to, he eventually realised that it was no longer appropriate. He had to fundamentally change his thinking.

The paradigm and role of HR is dictated, to a great extent, not by HR people but by the mental models of MDs and managers who have a view on how best to organise and manage their workforce. These models are an amalgam of a whole host of assumptions, both explicit and implicit, about what makes people tick, personal values, morality and different management philosophies.

So, for example, are line managers expected to 'manage' on their own? Is there a general belief that the morale of the workforce is important? Are HR activities supposed to focus on keeping the workforce happy or are individual and organisational performance the main objectives? More interestingly, are 'workforce happiness' and organisational performance conflicting objectives?

Rather than run through all the multitude of variations on the theme of HR paradigms, consider the two models shown in Figure 1.2 below. The model on the left suggests that HR should focus its attention on employee satisfaction, morale and motivational matters in an effort to support performance improvements. The one on the right suggests that HR should focus, first and foremost, on business goals and then put in place effective HRM practices that will motivate employees to achieve those goals. If these HR practices work, the outputs required will be achieved, performance will improve and this will engender greater organisational morale.

Either model could be applied and, although they are both endeavouring to improve performance, their starting points and thrust are entirely different. In the employee-focused model, morale is seen as a cause of performance. In the goal-focused model, improved organisational effectiveness is the cause of increased morale.

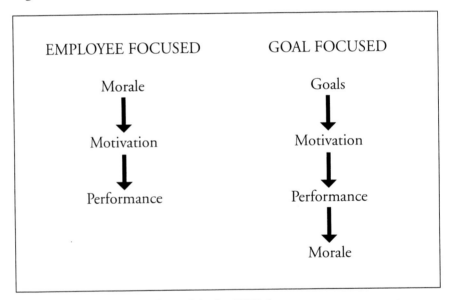

Figure 1.2 Two mental models for HRM.

What difference does the adoption of the chosen model make in practice? Stress management has become an industry in its own right as a result of the relentless pressure on organisations these days. So what should an HR team do to help deal with this problem? If they use the employee-focused morale model they try to deal with the symptoms of employee stress first. So they send these employees on stress management courses.

Those who adopt the goal-focused model, however, deal with the underlying, root causes of stress. They look at the most effective (and least stressful?) ways of achieving the organisation's goals. They focus on performance and work with employees to help them perform without getting too stressed out.

Here is a good example of what happens using the first model. Look at this snippet from *Personnel Today*, 5 November 1998. Under the heading 'Stress puts the NHS [National Health Service] in critical condition' it reports that the Head of Human Resources at Aintree Hospitals in the UK said: "'It puts us in human resources under stress because everyone looks to us for an answer. But we do not have one.'" The article continues: 'Aintree has a team of 10 counsellors, holds stress management training courses and runs a bullying and harassment phone line, yet the trust said it is still having little impact on stress levels.'

Dealing with symptoms never eradicates the disease. You would have thought that the NHS, more than any other organisation, would have learned this lesson by now.

Similarly, I have heard managers saying, on many occasions, that training is a great morale booster and this is their sole justification for requesting the training, even though they have no idea how this will help to achieve business goals. Yet, when pressed, such managers will usually agree that they hope for a performance improvement at some, albeit indeterminate, point in the future. Obviously the main question is, should this type of 'training' happen at all?

The bottom line HR function uses the goal-focused model: *everything the bottom line HR function does should start with a question about the goals of the organisation.* This may not be easy to do but lack of effort at this first stage undermines the whole process. Only when the goals are clear can the question of motivation be addressed. In fact, giving employees clear goals and direction, in this model, is a key motivational factor. Here the causal relationship suggests motivation is an effect of clarity. In the other model there is a belief that motivation, in itself, is a key driver of performance.

This is just an illustration of the different mental models we all work to. We are often not completely aware that we have a mental model or have chosen a particular model. Whichever one we use, though, naturally or consciously, it is based on some very deep-seated values and an unshakeable belief system.

As with all belief systems, you challenge them at your peril. People can feel very insecure and get aggressive when they believe their cherished belief system is under threat. I am very conscious of this so, if your own belief system is starting to feel the adverse effects of a challenge, please bear with me for now. Don't forget Chuck Neilson became a 'born-again' HR guy.

The employee-focused model gives many managers a nice warm glow inside. They believe that they are genuinely putting the employees' interests first. They intuitively feel that high morale leads to high performance. Performance is the effect they want and morale and motivation are some of the main causes.

The goal-focused approach looks hard-nosed. Very few managers want to appear cold and callous. Here, the interests of the business always come before the interests of the individual employees. This, they believe, is likely to lead to dissatisfaction among employees and result in a lower performance. I think this is what lies behind Mike Judge's views on personnel versus HR.

There are, no doubt, a whole range of mental models that exist in managers' minds but the two offered here probably represent the main options. All others are likely to be on the same theme as one or the other. These models are incredibly important in HRM. The best model will provide a very sound basis for the management of people in the organisation. Choosing the wrong model will lead to very poor 'people management', as we will see later.

There are probably many reasons why these mental models lack clarity and do not provide a sound foundation for HRM. This is because we have to balance competing needs: the needs of the organisation and the needs of the individual. Knowing what both sides of the coin look like will help us to achieve a better balance and more clarity. Here are a few of the relevant 'coins' for you to consider:

- Employing people is a double-edged sword. Get employees on your side and the business can really move forward. On the other hand, upset the workforce and you could have industrial relations problems, poor cooperation or mediocre performance.

- It is a fact of organisational life that there has to be a degree of control exerted over everyone. Too much control and initiative is stifled; too little control and things can get out of hand.

- People are all unique individuals but the groups they work in can significantly influence their behaviour. You would like to reward the best performers but this might create discontent among the other members of the team.

- The organisation has to get results and these objectives take priority over all other considerations. Meanwhile many employees are following their own career agendas and the two may not coincide as much as you or they would like. Balancing individual needs with organisational needs can be difficult.

- You would like to treat your workforce as a valuable asset but the harsh realities of the commercial world, or pressures to cut costs, mean that they are as dispensable as any other resource.

Virtually every aspect of HRM has a positive and a negative side and maintaining the right balance is absolutely crucial. Knowing what balance you want is a matter of judgement. Keeping that balance is a matter of sending consistent and coherent signals and messages to the workforce regularly, over a long period of time. You can never reinforce these messages too much.

The last MD I worked for never understood this. Whenever we discussed health and safety issues he became a sanctimonious pillar of society who would never compromise on safety and would not countenance exposing any of our employees to unnecessary risks. Outside of his legal obligations though, any money needed to improve working conditions was always very begrudgingly and tardily spent.

Sometimes, within the same discussion, he would exhibit extreme views both 'for' and 'against' our workforce. So, having just hit the roof about us not providing the best quality safety equipment for them, he then cursed the workforce for complaining about the latest productivity targets. He did not seem to understand that maybe these two factors were connected in some way.

He never seemed to realise that employees can spot inconsistencies in management decisions a mile off. The workforce saw us as a management team who only did the bare minimum in terms of providing good working conditions that were safe. They also felt that our demands for greater productivity were always a case of 'all take and no give'. This minimised any goodwill we could have expected or engendered in the workforce and it also seriously limited our potential for improved business performance.

Unclear thinking means inconsistent decisions, which in turn means poor people management. Strategic HR looks at the whole employment package or deal. If the company cannot afford to provide spotless working conditions then it needs to accept this and communicate it to all employees. The downside is maybe an acceptance of higher wage rates or increasing staff turnover.

Changing perceptions of the role of HR

I think it was Tom Peters who said that 'perception is reality'. This does not mean that just because someone perceives there to be a bat in his or her attic there actually is a bat there. What he means is that our behaviour is dictated more by our perceptions than the actual reality of the situation. So, if you think there is a bat in your attic you may go up there to get rid of it or just sit there too frightened to confront it. Either way, your perception is your reality until someone gets rid of the bat or proves that it does not exist.

If I am a senior manager and my perception of training is that it is not that important, do not be surprised if I do not want my staff away from their desks on training programmes. Or, if we suddenly have an operational crisis I may pull my people out of the training room because my immediate need is more important than their training. This type of perception leads to a lose/lose situation.

Maybe the operational crisis has resulted from a lack of training in the first place, so this is now a vicious circle. Training policies try to ensure the right training for the right people at the right time. HRM sees the bigger picture and builds into its calculations the need to re-educate the operational manager who has an outmoded perception of the value of training. HRM also tries to ensure that time is built into operational schedules to allow training to take place. It also does a great deal more but this will suffice for illustrative purposes for the time being.

Needless to say, if there is a perception that HR is 'faddish', then those who hold this perception are just waiting for the fad to fade, as Geoff Armstrong suggests. To avoid this happening a great deal of work has to be done to alter perceptions. The aim is to achieve a common understanding about HR's role by everyone in the organisation. This takes some doing but in Chapter 2 we will show how to align the various perceptions that can and do exist.

Notes

1. Dave Ulrich (1998) 'A new mandate for human resources', *Harvard Business Review*, January/February.

2. John Storey (ed.) (1995) *Human Resource Management: A Critical Text*. London: Routledge.

CHAPTER 2

Where are you on the HRM scale of effectiveness?

The HRM scale of effectiveness

Figure 2.1, at first glance, may look a little impenetrable. That is because it tries to convey many ideas in one simple graphic. I have often thought about breaking it down into two or three separate components but have come to the conclusion that this would belie the true, holistic nature of HRM. You cannot look at the subject just as a set of separate parts. It is either a whole or it is nothing. We will come back to the idea of HRM being intrinsically holistic but for now regard this diagram as a continuum. It is meant to be a representation of many perspectives on personnel and HR. Let us look at each of them in turn but, at the same time, try to keep the total picture in our minds.

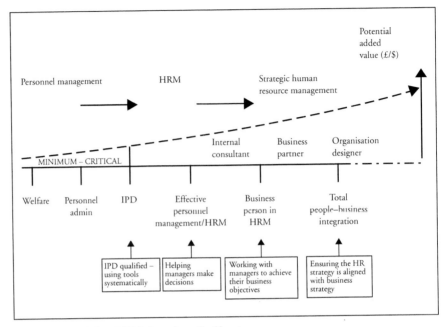

Figure 2.1 The HRM scale of effectiveness.

The historical evolution of HRM

Without going into the history of HR in too much detail it could be said that this scale, or continuum, shown in Figure 2.1 represents the historical evolution of the function. It originally started as a welfare function (one of the precursors of the IPD was the Institute of Welfare Officers in the early part of the last century). Over time, those involved in this sort of work took on more and more administrative tasks to do with employment so the idea of personnel administration developed.

As the role of personnel expanded so did the need for professionalism. This probably just started with having decent application forms but moved on to much more sophisticated tools and techniques such as psychometric tests for recruitment and selection purposes. Inevitably, the professional institute tended to become the arbiter of professionalism and practitioners could become IPD qualified.

Jumping ahead quite a few years, the whole question of linking people strategies to the business strategy became the 'Holy Grail' in HR circles. It has to be said this is much easier said than done, but there has been general agreement that this is the ultimate aim of HR.

However, while we can take a broad view of the historical development of the function this does not mean that the HR function has developed uniformly across all organisations. There is a very wide range of stages of development evident in organisations, even between those in the same industry. Also, one only has to look at the relatively recent introduction of some of the more progressive HR activities into the public sector to realise that certain sectors are only just beginning to address the issue of HR strategy and how to link it to business strategy.

This historical perspective does, however, start to introduce some important considerations. For example, older and maybe more senior managers will remember personnel as an entirely administrative function. Their perception of the work usually done by personnel people and the current needs of their organisation could be miles apart. So there is the issue of historical 'baggage'.

Furthermore, the people who worked in personnel some years ago were a very different breed to the more modern personnel practitioner. It was not unusual for the head of personnel to be an avuncular old manager who had passed their sell-by date in terms of operational effectiveness, yet the organisation valued their knowledge of the business and the people in it. It was also not uncommon (and surprisingly remains so today) for the MD's personal assistant, particularly in growing businesses, to be given responsibility for the more confidential personnel files and to eventually grow into the head of personnel role.

So a sense of history and an understanding of where personnel came from and where it is today are all very important when looking at its contribution.

HRM is inherently strategic, personnel isn't

If we return to the personnel versus HRM debate though, just for a moment, the scale in Figure 2.1 shows an evolutionary development from personnel management through HRM to strategic HRM. This not only represents my view of where HRM came from but also indicates that personnel management is just a subset of strategic HRM. Most of the work of personnel management is administrative. Yes, we could call it HR administration but let us not add further terminological confusion.

However, some personnel departments are just that and no more. They have no one sitting on the board and their most senior person is themselves, bogged down in day-to-day operational personnel matters. The best they can hope to be is very responsive to the needs of the business. However, reactive is a better description of their modus operandi. So, for example, they may suddenly have to find a lot of new recruits to fulfil the latest contract, which no one had bothered to tell them about in advance.

So while the debate about personnel versus HR continues to rage, the true position and role of the 'HR' function will be of paramount importance. This means that, regardless of what a function decides to call itself, personnel or HR, in reality most 'HR' functions are really nothing more than personnel administration departments.

So where are you on the scale?

I normally say to personnel and HR people 'where are you on this scale?' – and, by the way, it is intended to be a cumulative scale. Modern welfare policies, for instance, may not move the organisation very far forward on their own, but they will still be an integral part of an overall HR strategy.

But if the role is, primarily, stuck at the lower end of the scale, performing a traditional administrative function, then the name of the game just becomes efficiency. The only questions here are all to do with the costs, time and possibly internal customer satisfaction (i.e. line management) associated with the fulfilment of these basic tasks.

If people really *are* the only source of competitive advantage left, though, then the extent to which HR is acting strategically to manage this resource is of much greater interest and has the potential to add much more value. One only has to consider the different ways in which Japanese and western organisations have managed their employee relations to see, absolutely clearly, the impact such strategic HR decisions can have on organisational performance.

Unfortunately, while high added value is an exciting prospect for HR, the opposite side of the coin is risk. So, being the first company in a particular industry to remove union recognition might bring substantial benefits, but to achieve it would require managing a high degree of risk.

For now, though, let us look at each point on the scale in a little more detail.

Welfare and personnel administration to IPD

First, from an entirely functional point of view, is personnel just seen as a welfare function, making sure staff are looked after when they are off sick or have personal problems? Or, is it an administration function, making sure that recruitment advertisements show the company logo and that new starters have contracts? Or has it developed enough professional expertise (through IPD qualified staff) to offer psychometric assessment of new staff before they are offered a job?

The theory of this scale suggests that, as they move along the continuum, the function will add more value. Maybe a professionally qualified personnel team have better recruitment methods than a purely administrative team, ensuring a higher percentage of new recruits are well selected. This might mean they stay with the company for a reasonable amount of time. This reduces recruitment costs and improves average performance levels. Hence the more professional the team the more value they add.

Most personnel teams would want to at least have reached the 'IPD' level on the scale, for obvious reasons, until I point out to them that this means they are only about one-third along the scale. Also, they are still just carrying out a minimum, albeit critical, role. Furthermore, they are admitting they are only doing what all other IPD qualified people are doing, so none of them has gained a competitive advantage. When explained this way it does not sound so impressive, does it? This leads many of them to suggest that they are actually further along the scale than they originally claimed, but they rarely sound convinced.

Effective personnel management

Up to the IPD point on the scale, the personnel team are really only dealing with work as it arises, in a reactive way. To be an effective personnel manager they have to be much more proactive. If we stick with the recruitment example for now, this means that, rather than waiting for the vacancy notification to arrive on their desks, they should be out of their office much more with their ear to the ground, picking up any rumours about people who are looking for jobs elsewhere. This is a higher added value role because they may be able to anticipate vacancies and so have new recruits available sooner, meaning less disruption for the business. They may even take avoiding action to stop losing key people.

You may have noticed that we have slipped from talking about the HR function, per se, to looking at individual roles in the HR team. This is inevitable. Two recruitment officers working in the same HR team can adopt very different roles. One just waits for work to pile up on their desk and does the work they have to. The other is getting much more involved with line managers and even being asked to advise on recruitment decisions, even though, on paper, they do exactly the same job.

So where *you* are on this scale is actually a much more personal question than it seemed at first. Those who choose to make HRM their career come into it with a wide range of interests and aspirations. Generally, we all tend to choose the role that suits us best. So administrators choose administration, effective personnel managers choose a role where they can have more effect.

I have never seen any research which purports to describe the psychological profile of your normal, run-of-the-mill personnel manager but my own experience of meeting and talking to literally thousands of them is that the majority are very well intentioned and are 'interested in people' (whatever that means). However, no one would describe them as movers and shakers. If they were, they probably would have chosen a different career path.

Don't ask me why I came into HR. It is still a mystery to me, but I have stayed with it, in spite of the fact that I believe it has to fundamentally change. This probably means I must still enjoy working in the profession, or at least my version of it.

I will say, though, with as much authority as I can muster, that one attribute or trait that is definitely missing in the average personnel person's make-up is assertiveness. Because they are nice people they tend to want to avoid conflict and confrontation. Unfortunately, they now work in a function that has to be a driver of organisational change. This inevitably leads to handling conflict and confrontation and, although they may have many skills of tact and diplomacy, the one thing you cannot do is walk away from the issue of confronting and overcoming obstacles to change. To move along the scale of effectiveness automatically means personnel people need to be more assertive.

On a training programme I attended many years ago for my certificate in training competence, I had spent several weeks with other budding trainers from a wide variety of organisations. Every day in the hotel where we were based, we would have our own buffet lunch set out in the restaurant, just for the participants on our programme. On the very day that we had covered the importance of assertiveness on our programme we adjourned to the restaurant for our buffet lunch, as usual, only to find a long queue of elderly people already tucking into our food. There was immediate consternation in our group and mumblings about the cheek of it all, but no one went to speak to the elderly coach party. Instead, we just stood there watching helplessly as the pile of food rapidly diminished in front of our very eyes.

After a minute or so I suggested to some of my colleagues that this was a good test of whether we had learned to be more assertive. To prove the point I promptly went to the head of the queue to announce that they were feeding at the wrong table. Even I probably blushed but my intervention was just in time to save enough of the food intended for us. Perhaps you can train people in assertiveness but you only know they are trained properly when they get results.

Just to finish on this particular aspect of the scale, it is worth pointing out that most HR functions will have a variety of HR people in them. The head of the HR function has to decide what sort of people they want in their team and the roles they need to play. However, they also have to take on board what everybody else in the organisation wants from HR. It is all right having administrators in the team as long as the organisation needs administration. The problems arise when the organisation cannot afford to have mere administrators. The administrators themselves also have to be aware that they are always going to be under threat when their role adds very limited value.

While we are working our way along the scale it is interesting to stop and look at the scale from the viewpoint and perceptions of others outside the HR function.

The line manager's perception of HR

So far we have only looked at the HR practitioner's perception of their role. What if the line manager's perception of personnel is that all they just want them to do is arrange recruitment advertisements, pass on the application forms and CVs and leave them to make all the decisions? Such line managers do not want HR people sticking their noses in where they are not wanted. They do not value their contribution.

Becoming assertive is therefore not all personnel people have to do. They have to be able to demonstrate how they add value to the selection process. They need knowledge and skills that the line manager does not possess and must develop a positive working relationship. This is not 'muscling in' on the line manager's territory but helping them to make better decisions and showing them that one plus one equals three, by proving that better decisions have come about as a result.

I have worked with many line managers who held very outdated views on what they could expect from HR. In one case two senior engineers, used to making their own decisions, did not really want my involvement. So I agreed that they should manage the selection process, for a middle-ranking engineering vacancy, but offered to help with the final interviews. When the day for the final interviews arrived the engineering director let slip that he and his colleague already had a favourite candidate and just wanted me to rubber stamp their selection. About five minutes into the interview with this individual I was methodically working my way through the applicant's CV when it became pretty obvious that the CV was a total fabrication. The senior engineers had not even bothered to check the details and were sold on the candidate's natural bonhomie and easy-to-get-on-with nature. Nevertheless, they thanked me afterwards for stopping them making a big mistake.

This is not an argument for HR taking over. It takes two to tango properly and there is definitely an argument that effective HR professionals, working closely with the line, produce better decisions than either side working in isolation. Whether this relationship will happen in practice is dependent on two key factors. First, the HR practitioner must want it to happen and have the expertise and credibility to make it happen. Second, the head of HR must have established this role for HR in the minds of the board and managers, which is part and parcel of developing an effective HR strategy.

The business person in personnel

Becoming an effective personnel manager is just starting to cross the boundary between personnel and HRM. I have seen some highly effective personnel managers working in an environment where there is no effective HR strategy, so I would describe their work as coming under the HRM banner. The next boundary to cross is to that of 'businessperson in personnel' (BiP), otherwise known in my lexicon as an HR manager. This is another significant step along the scale.

BiP is not a brilliant title for this role but I continue to use it because it is meant to signify a fundamental shift in mindset. I also call myself a businessman first and an HRM professional second. However, I will revert to HR manager from now on.

Many personnel practitioners do not actually see their role as a 'business' role. They feel that somehow they sit outside of the mainstream operation of the organisation. This perception is also shared by many senior managers, whose perception of personnel is a support service that they only use when they need it. HR is never uppermost in their mind, except when the tribunal application lands on their desk.

The HR manager has to have a mandate to work with line managers on achieving business objectives. There is a shift here because the HR manager now has a *right* to get involved and have access to the same information as the operational manager. Of course, systems have to be put in place to back this up. So the recruitment or salary increase authorisation form has to have the HR manager's signature on it. There is also another fundamental shift in the line manager/HR manager relationship though.

Let us return to the recruitment example. The discussion with the manager does not start by looking at a vacancy that has just arisen, or even when there is an anticipation of a vacancy occurring. Instead, the thrust of the discussion centres on the manager's ability to deliver their business objectives. Have they got the right people in the right jobs? Where are the pressure points and the weaknesses in the team? Which objectives might they fail to deliver? This is HRM definitely moving onto the sacred ground of the traditional manager.

You can see immediately that the relationship between the HR manager and the line manager has moved on. The HR manager may be described more as an *internal consultant* or even a *business partner*. The *consultant* focuses on the business needs but is still mainly advising and offering expertise. The *business partner* is a totally equal relationship, even if on paper the manager has greater seniority.

In practical terms, this means that the 'business partner' HR manager has access to all of the information that the manager is privy to. If there is a disagreement between them the HR manager has recourse to a higher level of adjudication, whether through the HR director or someone equally senior in a line role. An unassertive HR manager would not survive in this role for long.

The internal consultant/HR manager has expertise that no line manager can possess because much of the advice will be of a specialist nature. This might be in-depth knowledge of the implications of employment legislation or state-of-the-art assessment techniques. The HR manager is confident in this role; they have to speak with authority and, ultimately, be prepared to share accountability with the line manager for any decisions that are taken. The downside of added value is risk. The proactive HR manager, who potentially adds a great deal of value, has to accept that they are now entering into a riskier world. If the new recruit does not work out it is as much down to them as it is to the line manager.

Many existing personnel professionals do not aspire to or have the ability to be true HR managers in the business partner sense. They also do not welcome risk.

Organisation designer

We are now moving to the extreme right-hand side of the scale in Figure 2.1 – the highest added value end of the scale, the riskiest end of the scale. Probably the highest value HR activity is in the area of organisation design. The HR manager can talk about the strengths and weaknesses in a team. The organisation designer knows how to redesign teams, departments and functions. They have in-depth knowledge of processes and organisation structures and the interrelationship between the two. They have to be extremely articulate to be able to express difficult concepts and they need the powers of persuasion to convince senior people to change the way they organise their territory.

They know the pros and cons of flexible structures and matrix organisations. They understand how to balance the need for managerial control with allowing people the freedom to act. They appreciate the difficulties associated with increasing someone's responsibilities and accountability and they have the political nous to realise the art of the possible.

The effective organisation designer is worth their weight in gold. The bad organisation designer may pose one of the biggest risks that your organisation has ever faced. This lesson had to be learned by some organisations that jumped on the business process re-engineering bandwagon. A colleague of mine often relates the story of the Australian bank which removed several layers of managers only to find later that the bad debt ratio had risen sharply as a result. The process of sifting out potentially bad business resided in the many years of experience of some of the very managers they felt they could discard.

It takes a long time to become a good organisation designer. The textbooks can only teach you a very small part of what is required. An academic lecturer I met, who was introduced to me as the 'organisation specialist', was unable to show me a book that would explain 'how to do it'. He quoted several learned and standard academic texts which surveyed what organisations did, but even he admitted that such texts would not give the practitioner much help in their new job tomorrow. He could not even recommend any guidelines on matters such as 'what would be a normal span of control?' or 'what would be the maximum number of reports any manager should have?' These may be unfair questions but they have to be answered by the practitioner.

One of my clients, a large multinational communications company, had just reorganised itself. The board comprised 15 members, with some heading up their own functions. I had no hesitation in advising my client, the HR director, that this was far too many for this particular business. He agreed and went on to describe how at least five of them were only there because the MD had not got around to biting the bullet on the ones that they did not need anymore.

An effective HR director, who is also a good organisation designer, would have made sure the MD had bitten the bullet. If they failed to do so, then one of their greatest opportunities to add significant value to this business had been sidestepped, and I am not just talking about a saving in salaries. Board directors who should not be there are getting in the way of progress.

There is a serious shortage of people in the HR world at the moment with the necessary skills to fulfil this role. This will seriously hamper the HRM profession's attempts to operate at a truly strategic level.

High- and low-value activity in HR

As a writer and public speaker I am always looking out for good analogies to get a particular point across. Just the other day, I was listening to the radio and John Bird, a well-known satirist in the UK, was telling a story about his partner who is a concert pianist. At one concert, the 'page turner' for the pianist failed to show up and John Bird was asked to stand in at the last minute. The interviewer asked him whether he had managed to do a good job or not. He replied, 'Well, no one ever asks whether the page-turner was any good or not, the audience just expects that to be perfect. It's the quality of the music they come to hear.'

This is a brilliant analogy for personnel officers. They are the page-turners of industry. No one ever wants to focus on their page-turning ability, unless of course they get it badly wrong.

The importance of this point is that we need to know which HR activities really matter and which ones add the most value. I have alluded to 'value' several times already. Now we need to look at this concept in much more detail. However, I think the quotes below, which are both from the local authority sector, sum up the spectrum of value very succinctly.

In the magazine *People Management* on 20 April 1995 there was a report on the SOCPO (the Society of Chief Personnel Officers in UK local government) annual conference. Heather Rabbatts, the then Chief Executive of Lambeth Council, remarked:

> The personnel handbook of the future should be full of exciting examples of personnel people turning their organisation around, not grievance procedures.

At the same conference, the Personnel Department at Oldham Metropolitan Borough Council won that year's SOCPO award for innovation and achievement for its 'manual of standard employment-related letters'. Need I say more?

Added value is a very slippery concept and causes a great deal of confusion in HRM. You will notice in Figure 2.1 that there is a graph rising from left to right called 'Potential added value'. This graph tries to illustrate that of all the things HR can be doing, some activities are worth much more, in terms of value to the organisation, than others.

It is relatively easy to understand that a good, strategic HR decision (e.g. to develop your own managers rather than go out into the market) is likely to have much more of an impact on an organisation than an administrative activity (e.g. redesigning the company's application form). Therefore, HR functions that want to be high added value have to become strategic.

As I have already pointed out, though, the downside of high added value is risk. Any entrepreneur knows this. They generally get their biggest returns (or biggest losses) from their high-risk ventures. Messing up the design of the new application form is unlikely to be too disastrous; after all, it can always be reprinted. Strategic HR decisions, though, are not so easily undone. What happens if you lose all the managers you have just trained to a competitor whose HR strategy is to poach talent, at whatever cost?

A few years ago a large retail bank in the UK had just set up its own 24-hour phone banking service in response to their main competitor having stolen a march on them. At the same time this bank was shedding large numbers of staff as it ran down its high street branch operations. A decision was taken, therefore, to transfer some of the otherwise redundant staff to the new 24-hour call centre. This probably made sense on paper as it avoided high redundancy costs and placated the staff union.

You do not need to be an HR genius to work out that this was not a good strategic HR move. (I can only presume this bank did not have any good HR strategists.) Everyone knows that many banks have never been very customer focused and have spent many years breeding staff who regard the customer as a necessary evil. Putting such people into a brand new call centre operation, which had to be totally customer-oriented, was definitely a case of square pegs in round holes. It only took three months for them to realise their mistake and change their recruitment policy to ensure that no staff were transferred in from other parts of the branch business.

We will look at HR strategy in more detail in Chapter 7, but we should notice, straightaway, that Figure 2.1 really is a continuum in every sense of the word. A strategic decision about developing managers may also require basic paperwork changes by the personnel administration team. So the value of any activity cannot be gauged in isolation. Where an effective HR strategy is in place the changes to the application form become an important building block. Where there is no HR strategy in place this is just an exercise in printing new stationery which is about as valuable as the paper it is printed on.

Despite my earlier anecdote about the computer company's personnel department who did not *say* they added value, if you ask any personnel person, on a one-to-one basis, whether they believe their job is important or not, they will usually say it is. They would not be able to articulate this in any added value way but they do actually *think* they are adding lots of value already. Unfortunately, many are deluding themselves.

The paradox of low-value, critical HR activities

I deride many personnel departments because they are not adding a great deal of value. But that does not mean the work they do is not important. Quite the contrary – much of their work is critical. This is the paradox which causes so much confusion in HR circles, both within the profession itself and among its observers and critics.

Figure 2.1 is meant to reflect reality and, as so often happens, reality is very difficult for some to accept. Why? Because the scale is, in effect, saying that the vast majority of traditional personnel activities bring very little extra value to the organisation. The earlier reference to the use of psychometrics, a technique that has become a basic ingredient of the personnel practitioner's portfolio, can be used to demonstrate this point.

Recruitment officers are often fully trained and probably qualified to use a range of psychometric and other tools. They may have just become qualified in using, say, the OPQ or 16PF (both well recognised and well used psychometric tests) and will now feel much better qualified to do their job more effectively. What they tend to forget is that it will equally improve the effectiveness of all the other personnel officers on the same course who are now using the same tests.

So what is the value of their work? The recruiter, obviously, will argue that they add an enormous amount of value by making sure they assess and select the right people for the business. Intuitively, this argument has high face validity. However, it shows no understanding of the concept of added value, which always has a £ or $ sign attached.

Across the road is a competitor company, with an equally experienced recruiter, doing exactly the same things (I am not sure that necessarily means it must be 'best practice') and managing to recruit the right people. In other words, each recruitment officer's contribution to their respective employers is to ensure both companies compete on the same terms. In effect, good recruitment practices add no more *value* than ensuring each company has the latest specification computers on their desks.

If we had to put an actual £ or $ value on these HR activities all we could do is simply look at the total employment costs of the recruiters. This particular £/$ sign is not that impressive, based on normal salaries for personnel officers. Moreover, if they resigned tomorrow the company could get the same value simply by recruiting a replacement or just using an external provider or outsourcing company.

I am convinced that the use of psychometrics can genuinely improve selection and recruitment decisions. If this is true then these techniques should add value – and probably did when they were first introduced. But now that they are in general use it means, in practice, that standards of recruitment and selection have just moved up to a higher standard. Moreover, those who use them are all now still playing on a level, albeit higher, playing field. In such circumstances, none of them can gain an advantage over their competitors purely by using such tests. In other words these tests create no added value. This is not what hard-pressed personnel professionals want to hear.

This paradox of critical but low-value activity takes a bit of explaining. How can something that is critical to the operation of the business be of such low value? Well, personal computers are now critical to all businesses but they do not cost a fortune, do they? In HR terms another good example is industrial relations management.

Those actively involved in managing relations with unions (which used to include the author) may feel their role adds lots of value by resolving conflicts and generally improving employer/employee relations. But if their competitors do not have a union and do not have to spend time on this issue or pay for industrial relations specialists to manage workplace relations, it is difficult to see how such activity can be regarded as of any competitive advantage or value whatsoever.

Let us introduce the idea of benchmarking. From a benchmarking viewpoint, do you benchmark against organisations that have a similar industrial relations set-up or would it not be much more useful to look at the efficiency and effectiveness of organisations that do not have a union at all?

Undoubtedly, where the union continues to exist, mismanaging this relationship could have disastrous consequences through lack of cooperation, increased industrial action or stoppages. So, in this sense, the role is of critical importance. It has to be performed at a level that maintains the relations necessary for the organisation to continue to perform effectively. Usually, the 'minimum critical role' of personnel can only be valued in a negative sense. That is, what would the cost be if this role were not performed effectively? In this case, perhaps the potential cost of a crippling dispute.

You can always spot low-value activities because you never get patted on the back when you do them well. That is what you are expected to do. It is also worth noting that, despite being called a 'minimum' role, industrial relations actually takes up a great deal of time. It used to account for up to 90 per cent of my total working time when I was doing the job. So, while the minimum role takes up the major part of an HR function's time, the really high added value role can often be afforded less time than it should. We now start to really understand how HR's time and effort can often be focused in the wrong areas.

The highest added value role for HR has to be as the 'experts' in organisation design. This should be self-evident as it is only through the design of highly efficient and effective processes, melded creatively with flexible organisation structures, that organisations can provide a solid foundation for maximising the potential performance of individual employees, teams and the organisation itself. Alongside this is the need for a clear vision of how future employer/employee relationships are to be managed (not through a firefighting industrial relations manager). Furthermore, there should be a philosophy of creating a win/win situation for employer and employee, the two parties to this legal, economic and psychological contract.

Basic activities are critical when they support the HR strategy

About five years ago I was working with a UK hotel group that had just taken over a rival group. There was talk at senior levels about trying to merge and blend the cultures of the two organisations so that customers could expect a very high quality, seamless and consistent service. As part of these top-level discussions there was a cross-functional team looking at what they called 'training strategy'. Obviously, they anticipated that training and development activity would be needed to underpin and reinforce any culture shift (you can see how quickly and easily such discussions can become nebulous and unfocused).

I attended a meeting of this team, which included the HR director, the training director and a general manager from one of the hotels in the group that had just been bought. The body language and attitude of this general manager hinted that he was not really pleased to be part of the new group but he was doing his best to make a constructive contribution. However, as the talk turned to cultural issues I could see he was getting more and more irritated.

After about two hours of discussion that seemed to be going nowhere, he finally exploded:

> 'Don't talk to me about training strategy and how to get my staff to change their attitudes. We had our first pay day from your [notice the word 'your'] payroll department last week and no one in my hotel got paid. You try talking to them about the advantages of working in the new, enlarged group and then ask them to change their attitudes. All they know at the moment is that you can't even pay your people on time!'

Needless to say this virtually brought the meeting to a standstill, and quite rightly so. Paying staff correctly and on time is a cardinal rule in personnel administration and woe betide anyone who fails to do so. This is a relatively simple activity which most of us take for granted. It is only when it goes badly wrong that it causes ructions. In these particular circumstances it meant a great deal of bridge building would now have to take place before the training strategy team could make progress towards their longer-term objectives.

The bottom line HR function knows that taking your eye off the ball on the basics can really undermine effective HR and business strategies.

In spite of all of this I still argue that payroll activity is of low value. How can this be so? The answer is relatively simple. In all of the companies I have worked for or with, none of them had a serious problem paying people. Yes, they had pay queries and the occasional glitch in the system but this did not seriously undermine the organisation. Running a payroll is not rocket science and no one would ever argue that their payroll department gives them a competitive edge. Also, salary levels are a good indicator of the value of any type of work and payroll managers do not earn a fortune.

Nevertheless, as in the case of the hotel group, getting payroll wrong at the wrong time shows just how important it is. This is why, on Figure 2.1, there is a whole area of work at the bottom end (the left-hand side) of the added value scale which has to be done to a set of minimum standards but which will never help the organisation move forward. What it can do, though, when it goes wrong, is hold the organisation back. That is why personnel have to get all of this work right. Otherwise their HR team will not be able to play with the big boys down at the strategic end of the scale.

Total people–business integration

The only item on the scale we have not mentioned so far is the idea of 'total people–business integration'. This is an aspiration as far as I am concerned. It is something akin to an organisational nirvana. The people who work in such organisations are totally focused on helping the organisation to fulfil its maximum potential. They are committed and hard-working because the organisation looks after them as well as it can. Words such as 'learning organisation' start to mean something because, while the employees are performing well, they are also learning all the time.

Personally, I do not know any organisation that fits this picture. The learning organisation, as a concept, was very popular a few years ago but I do not hear it mentioned much these days. This is probably because it was not fully understood, it was a little bit ahead of its time and, as usual, the HR people who jumped on this particular bandwagon jumped off again when they found something that sounded more sexy, like knowledge management or corporate university.

Let us just leave this end of the scale as an indeterminate goal for now. There is an awful lot of room for improvement in all HR functions before we need to worry too much about achieving total people–business integration.

Choose your HR role

If the scale is a true reflection of reality then what it sets out is a set of options for HR people. They can choose which is the role needed in their organisation and whether that is the role they want to play.

Many people who work in personnel, or came into the profession over ten years ago, still regard it as a support function and are quite happy in that role. They do not see it as a function that now has to make a greater, direct contribution to organisational performance. They do not think in terms of added value. As we have seen though, this mindset is becoming increasingly outmoded as organisations cannot afford to be complacent. They need to look for competitive advantage and added value wherever they can.

I often ask the personnel and HR people who come on my workshops and seminars 'where do you, personally, want to be on this scale?' If they are happy enough in a purely administrative role I usually reassure them that there is no problem with that as long as that is all the company expects from them. The problems arise when either the company expects more or decide that they can outsource the bottom end of the scale and save some money.

CHAPTER 3

The changing roles of HR

So what's wrong with HR managers?

In Chapter 1 we explored the awful reputation of personnel. Now we are moving on to consider why just 'managing' HR is not enough and try to illustrate the difference between HR 'management' and HR 'consulting'.

There are probably several key reasons why the role of many HR managers is no longer what is required in most organisations.

• HR managers have traditionally been seen as the servants of line management and have become involved in issues only when the line deemed it necessary. This was often too late for the HR manager to offer the most appropriate and effective advice and guidance. This is very neatly summed up by the typical example of the HR manager who has to manage a tribunal when earlier involvement could have avoided it altogether.

• Organisations struggling to cope with increasing competitive pressures cannot rely purely on the strengths of their managers to ensure that performance is maximised. Performance is a much broader issue than just managing operational tasks and there is a role for HR to ensure all aspects of performance are being handled effectively across the organisation. The line manager does not decide pay policy so can only manage performance within certain constraints.

- HR managers used to be the policy police. Now they have to ensure that HR strategy is put into effect. This has as much to do with reinforcing values and principles, over a sustained period, as it has to do with day-to-day activities.

- HR, as a subject, is now fully recognised as a much bigger and more complex arena. The 'science' of HR requires practitioners who can master new skills and knowledge and provide expertise. Specialist expertise automatically indicates a changing role for the erstwhile HR manager.

The demise of the HR generalist

The portfolio of skills, tools and techniques possessed by the HR manager of 20 years ago probably included, among many other things, a reasonable understanding of employment legislation, a basic qualification in psychometrics, an ability to design and run a rudimentary appraisal system and some experience of a proprietary job evaluation system.

The development of specialisms

Just looking at these four specific areas it is relatively easy to see how each of these has now developed into an entire specialism in its own right. Employment legislation has grown in size and complexity, particularly with the advent of EU legislation; training course provision is being augmented by a proliferation of development and assessment centres; appraisal is rapidly being supplanted by performance management systems and broad banding, a relatively new concept, is being introduced in an attempt to try and cope with a move towards more flexible jobs and payment systems.

When one compares the current situation with that of 20 years ago it is not too difficult to see that the HR manager of yesterday can now only be a jack-of-all-trades and, as we all know, a little knowledge can be a very dangerous thing. Modern, progressive organisations require HR people who have a profound understanding in all of the critical HR fields. This can only be achieved by employing specialists, whether they be internal or external.

It must not be forgotten, however, that personnel departments still have a mountain of administrative work to do. Often the HR manager who wants to work more closely with the line is severely constrained by day-to-day queries, paperwork and a welter of totally reactive activities which eat into the time they have available. So, although organisations need a more valuable contribution from their HR managers, they often do not provide sufficient resources to enable their HR managers to get away from their desks.

HR costs and resourcing are big issues

The whole issue of realising what changes are necessary in HR is clouded by confusion in many business leaders' minds concerning the distinction between personnel administration and the very different role that HR can play. Personnel administration, while necessary, is a time-consuming and costly activity with no obvious return on investment. HR, on the other hand, should be focused on contributing added value rather than just being seen as another cost centre.

In practice, the total HR/personnel function is provided with a budget that does not truly reflect the split between added value and cost-only activities. Worse still, the demands of the personnel role, in both time and money, soak up much of the HR function's resources (see Appendices E and F). Hence, resourcing of HR is often inappropriately weighted in favour of low-value personnel activities. In effect, this means HR managers are trying to do the job with one hand tied behind their backs.

Cost-driven finance executives view much of personnel's work as cost-only activities without a corresponding return on investment. So the only course they want to follow is to try and find the cheapest supplier of these services. Although this view could be criticised as a short-sighted and misguided view of the importance of personnel administration it, nevertheless, is currently driving an increasing number of organisations to seriously consider the outsourcing option.

Admittedly, outsourcing the 'commodity' activities of payroll, pensions and some areas of recruitment and training may bring efficiencies but cost is only one side of the equation. A more positive approach is to handle administration efficiently enough to then divert resources into HR.

Against this backdrop, the days of the generalist HR manager could well be numbered unless they simultaneously start changing the focus of their work and shifting perceptions of what they can achieve. This will involve a certain amount of reinvention and re-education.

When is an HR manager an HR consultant?

A key part of reinventing the HR manager's role is to turn them into internal consultants. However, saying it is easy but what exactly does it mean in practice? HR managers become consultants when they drop the jack-of-all-trades tag. The consultant's role is inherently one that involves expertise in one or more specialisms. No doubt HR managers would like to think that they keep reasonably abreast of all the latest developments but few would be able to develop true expertise in more than perhaps a couple of these areas in the short term.

HR has always been a function to which the line turns for advice, whether it be on employment terms and conditions, training or disciplinary matters. Some may have always regarded this as inherently a consultancy role. But is it? What are the fundamental differences between being an HR manager and acting as a consultant?

If we look to the role of external HR consultants as a point of reference, we tend to see specialisms such as job evaluation, pay systems, specific training and development fields, psychological assessment and employee communications. In other areas, such as employment law, this is now often contracted out to an employment law specialist or a solicitor. Each area is regarded as a discrete subject that can be separated out from the rest of the HR portfolio.

Specialist HR consultants are normally only called in when a specific need arises. They may develop a very close working relationship with their clients but another consultant can always stand in if necessary. Even if the external consultants get involved with line or senior management they will normally be viewed as standing outside the organisation and, with the best will in the world, will not be expected to have an intimate knowledge of the culture and workings of the organisation.

So would an *internal* HR consultant essentially fulfil the same role? This begs several questions.

Let us look at the subject of job evaluation. Traditionally, the initial decision to have a felt-fair and systematic approach to pay and grading led to the popularity of job evaluation and, in particular, the Hay system. Once the decision was made to use Hay their consultants would often instigate the whole process and the local HR manager was expected to ensure the integrity of the system on their patch. As part of this role the HR manager would advise line managers on the job evaluation system and may actually undertake any further job analyses.

Both the external consultant and the internal HR manager have a consultancy role; one is the specialist on the system the other has the knowledge and experience of applying it in the workplace. But to what extent has consultancy really taken place?

If we look at a similar situation today, the internal HR consultant should be asking questions like 'what sort of pay system do we want? how flexible do our grading structures need to be? how much are we targeting our resources towards the people that really contribute?' Perhaps the application of a proprietary evaluation system is no longer an appropriate solution in an organisation where performance and flexibility now take precedence over the need for consistency.

HR managers cannot and should not be single-solution consultants. They must understand the context of their own business and work within a coherent, strategic framework. They must have their own areas of particular expertise but also know enough about other specialisms to be able to call on them when they deem it necessary.

HR internal consultancy is higher added value work than personnel administration and is a full-time job. However, to find enough time to do the job properly means initially finding the 'headroom', as one of my clients called it, to shift from reactive work to proactive consultancy. Over a period of time the HR function needs to be resourced sufficiently to enable this to happen.

Consultant, adviser or business partner?

Being clear about the actual internal HR consultant concept is very important but, without being too pedantic, terminology is very important as well. When is a 'consultant' not a consultant, for example? Perhaps one answer to this is 'when they are just an adviser'.

Advisers are asked for their advice, consultants are more involved in the decision-making process. For example, an HR manager/adviser might be asked to help design a selection procedure for filling a vacancy. An HR consultant, on the other hand, would be involved in the very early stages of discussions about exactly what vacancy exists. Moreover, they would consider a range of other possible solutions including changing the roles of the rest of the team or completely reconfiguring the team itself.

The HR manager as business partner is a different role again. Here the partner is working closely with the operational departmental head and looking at the best options available for achieving current and future business objectives. This is a very equal relationship, with the partner knowing as much about the business as the departmental head. Also, the partner is totally aware of the rest of the business and takes this into consideration when helping to formulate a solution. For example, could the work required be undertaken more efficiently or effectively by another section or team?

So the internal HR consultant sits somewhere between HR managers who advise and those who act as business partners. This, and all the other HR roles we have identified, are plotted on the graph in Figure 3.1. A combination of the capability of the role holder and their personal levels of proactivity and credibility determine the position of each role. In addition, there is a further indication of the relative value of each of these roles.

Personal credibility and authority

One thing that ambitious and committed HR people have to do is develop their own personal credibility and authority. This is probably true of any professional position but perhaps HR has more of a hill to climb because of persistent, outdated perceptions of HR as the sort of bureaucracy Thomas Stewart was referring to in Chapter 1.

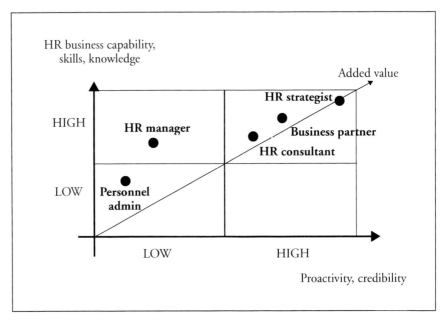

Figure 3.1 High added value HR roles.

Obviously a certain amount of credibility comes with a high degree of professionalism but there are many other personal attributes that the HR consultant has to exhibit. We referred earlier to the need for personal assertiveness which, again, is a prerequisite of developing a higher degree of proactivity.

Line managers do not always see the relevance of an experienced HR perspective on what may appear to them to be an operational problem. Their perception of the 'difficult' employee might be that it is an 'open and shut' disciplinary case. Having to consider all the factors that contributed to the behaviour of this individual, and how they might help to resolve it, may seem more trouble than it is worth.

If the HR consultant cannot ensure that the manager takes on board such considerations then they will just slip back into their reactive hiring, firing and support role.

Another aspect of proactivity is all to do with establishing the HR consultancy role itself. If the consultant has to become involved with real business issues then awkward questions may have to be asked about the manager's ability to achieve their own business objectives (and, indeed, whether they are absolutely clear what their own objectives are!). This can look like the HR consultant is meddling in affairs that are of no concern to them. A firm line has to be taken to help educate management that this is certainly within the remit of the HR consultant's role.

An excellent example of this point happened to me when I was involved in discussion with an HR director and I started asking tough questions about the company's financial situation. My client decided to invite his finance director to join us. When he did I immediately put my questions to him regarding the profitability of the business and the current key business issues. With a perplexed look the finance director remarked 'Why do *you* want to know that? I thought you were a personnel consultant?'

Becoming an HR consultant is as much to do with getting other managers to meet you at least half way as it is to do with developing your own expertise. The whole relationship with the business has to fundamentally shift.

Changing relationships

Historically, the HR function has had to constantly change its relationship with the line. The industrial relations managers of the 1960s and 1970s had to become the employee relations managers of the 1980s and 1990s. The job analyst's role has undergone several metamorphoses through job evaluation to become what is now the role of competence analyst.

These are not just changes in job role, or even skills and knowledge. They represent a fundamental shift in the perceptions of and actual relationship between HR practitioners and the managers they work with. They are no longer called in by the line 'as and when required' to pick up the pieces but have had to become an integral part of the whole management process.

HR managers, for too long the servants of the line and having to operate in an entirely reactive fashion, should be viewed as consultants whose skills and knowledge will help to solve complex, and often intractable business problems that require intelligent, HR-based solutions. At its best this relationship is characterised by an HR manager who is so proactive that they are raising issues with the line long before the line managers themselves have identified any potential problems looming on the horizon.

Recently, an insurance broking organisation in the UK was desperately trying to improve its very poor cost/income ratio and had embarked on a whole range of 'change' activities, including trying to train well-established managers to manage their teams more effectively.

Here, the HR manager's contribution was purely to make sure standard training programmes took place. An effective HR consultant would have highlighted the fact that this business did not fully acknowledge the fundamental shift needed in the way it handled its business. This in turn needed new people with new skills, working in a different style within well-designed, efficient processes. No one in the business made the right HR connections and fully understood the people implications of what they were trying to achieve.

In reactive mode the HR manager's contribution was to ensure that badly designed and, therefore, ineffective policies would be implemented. In proactive mode, as consultants, their contribution would have been of immense value in reducing operating costs while at the same time ensuring that any HR fallout was planned for, and dealt with, effectively.

In organisations where HR is underdeveloped – and probably undervalued as a discipline – then it is probably perceived only as a personnel administration function. There is little chance that HR managers in this environment could embark on developing a consultancy role for themselves with much likelihood of success.

CHAPTER 4

Changing HR and management mindsets

Business-focused HR people

The case for HR managers to act as consultants is relatively easily made. However, there has been an implicit assumption so far that HR managers want to act as consultants. This cannot be taken for granted so readily.

The nature of those who entered the profession 20 or so years ago may have been very well suited to the role that HR then held. This included a desire to offer professional, some would say 'off-the-shelf', personnel solutions such as the Hay evaluated pay and grading systems mentioned in the previous chapter. Being 'professional' meant being qualified but there was less involvement in the day-to-day management of the organisation.

Now, if HR is meant to be as business-focused as any other part of the organisation, it is inevitably working at the coalface more than in its ivory tower. Hence, those who want to continue working in the function have to be prepared to get their hands dirty and, more importantly, share some of the risk. One has to ask the question, therefore, are these the sort of traits that one normally associates with conventional HR people?

Equally, if organisations really do need good HR consultants, then are senior and middle managers prepared to accept what that means in terms of their own authority and status? Are managers prepared to be questioned closely about how they intend to achieve business objectives? Are senior managers willing to be challenged about their business strategy and how it impacts on people in the organisation?

We keep coming back to this issue of assertiveness. One of the main reasons that they have to assert themselves is that getting to grips with the really tough HR issues of managing performance, handling pressure and stress and doing more with less means telling managers that traditional methods of managing are no longer appropriate. The HR consultant has to be able to convince managers that they, themselves, have to change their mindset.

The prime role of personnel

So we can see that there is a range of roles for HR functions and the people who work in them. Within the role though there is a wide range of jobs that HR has to fulfil. In fact there is no other function that wears as many hats as HR and I think I have personally worn them all at one time or another.

These include being the 'industrial social worker' having to deal with staff whose home lives disrupt their working lives, with partners walking out or kids playing truant. Or the 'tea and sympathy dispenser' for an employee who is going through a particularly bad divorce and needs somebody to speak to (and would not dream of talking to their boss about it).

What about the role of 'equal rights campaigner' for the woman who really deserves consideration for the promotion that her male colleague is in line for? Or the 'Dutch uncle' when you have to have a quiet word with somebody about their behaviour or the fact they have just upset one of the directors?

As someone who started their professional life as an industrial relations specialist I identified many roles in this particular field ranging from 'macho man negotiator' to 'organisational oil can', keeping the wheels in motion and acting as the conciliator, and even 'legal eagle' who had to know whether what we were doing was within the law.

The worst hat that I have ever had to wear, though, was the one that my last MD tried to foist on me. He used to refer to me as the 'conscience of the organisation'. It was as though all other functional heads could take decisions based on the grounds of cold, calculated, commercial needs while I was expected to look after the human fallout, or at least constantly make these managers aware of the human implications of their hard-nosed decisions.

This awful, cringe-making title suggested to me that my MD did not know the first thing about HRM and probably had very conflicting views about what he expected from it. This was particularly surprising because he started out life as a personnel manager himself. He also did not like the term HRM.

Here is another fundamental problem for the HR function. This welter of roles often means that it is very difficult to reconcile them all. How, for example, does an HR manager reconcile the following roles:

• employee counsellor for the stressed out employee;

   with

- overseer of the disciplinary procedure where they might have to issue a warning;

  and

- performance manager trying to maximise employee performance;

  with

- welfare worker for the employee who has become a long-term absentee.

With all of these different facets to the job what is the average employee's perception of the HR function, friend or foe? It is no wonder the HR profession is renowned for gazing at its navel interminably and constantly having identity crises.

I actually believe the answer to this particular conundrum is simple, but it is not easy to 'sell' either to the management team or employees at large.

We will continue to explore some of the many hats that HR people have to wear but there is one primary role that eclipses every other. *HRM's sole aim in life is to optimise the return from the organisation's human resource.* This does not mean flogging people to death. What it does mean is tapping into the full potential of the organisation's employees, at all levels. We can tap into this potential, partly by caring for employees, and partly by expecting a reasonable level of performance. There are always two sides to the coin, both of which are equally important but, as George Orwell would possibly say, the performance side is more equal.

The board's view of HR

At the end of the day, the only perception of HR's value that really matters is the board's perception. However, there is unlikely to be a consistent and coherent view held by all board members. In fact it amazes me how confused the picture seems to be at board level.

We are all used to hearing business leaders glibly referring to their people as being the organisation's greatest asset. Unfortunately, we are all equally cynical enough to know that this is, more often than not, just company rhetoric and public relations hype rather than a statement of any real substance.

My own view is that those who rise to the top of organisations rarely do so because of their ability to develop the people around them. This may be one of the biggest sweeping statements I am ever likely to utter (although there are probably quite a few other candidates for the title in this book) but it is certainly based on experience rather than theory.

Their career progression may have been down to hitting targets, brown-nosing, networking, good personal PR and a host of other factors. Along the way they may well have climbed up on the shoulders of many of their staff and colleagues who perhaps were not as ambitious, streetwise or politically astute. They certainly did not get where they are today by spending most of their precious time building and developing others.

These are not 'people' people by and large. Yes, there are probably many exceptions to this 'rule' but as someone who has spent many years thinking mainly from a HRM perspective it is unlikely that the directors of most organisations have put as much thought into this area. They may be very good at running a business based on most conventional measures of business success but, in terms of maximising the potential of their human resource, they are generally still in the starting blocks.

However, whether they have any natural inclination to understand the bigger HR issues or not, they ignore them at their peril. If my analysis of the situation is correct, they are poorly prepared for this role and a quick trip to any business school or management college is not going to change that overnight.

As a result of this, directors have to start thinking through, more clearly, exactly what their views on people management are. Often this leads to muddled thinking. So, for example, a board director will know that they may have certain legal responsibilities for health and safety or they might be genuinely worried about falling foul of equal opportunities or sexual harassment legislation. Consequently they will want to ensure they are well covered in these respects. They may also have a generally positive view that suggests employee motivation and morale should lead to improved organisational performance.

However, especially if they work in a unionised environment, they may well have more negative views on this subject or believe that many of their employees are lucky to have a job. What they are unlikely to have done is reconciled all of these, potentially conflicting views, into a unified, coherent view of strategic human resource management.

Amid all of this muddled thinking lurks an intuitive belief that much of the work of personnel administrators is of limited value. This is probably why the conventional wisdom is swinging round to outsourcing many of the day-to-day tasks of personnel such as payroll, basic recruitment and legal advice. Even if it is not outsourced, there is now a cost-saving drive to achieve economies of scale by running centralised 'HR service centres'.

This confused picture is not just a problem for senior HR practitioners but is also a very serious organisational issue, as we will see in Chapter 7 on HR strategy. One of the main aims of this book is to help business leaders to develop a clear and coherent view of how best to manage their human resource both in the short as well as the long term.

The employee's perception

Of all the different perceptions of HR's role, the employee's has to be dealt with last. Why? Because if the board do not have a coherent view then they will send all sorts of mixed messages to their workforce, one minute demanding performance improvements and more with less, the next minute instigating a culture change initiative which tries to alter managerial attitudes and behaviours. They might try to focus employees on their own contribution but still get more hung up about their timekeeping.

The HR department handles many management change initiatives, even if they do not own them. So, for example, it is the HR team that introduces the idea of 360° appraisal to enable a more open, honest and constructive dialogue to take place between managers and their staff. Any questions an individual might have on how the system works could well be handled by an HR person who tries to reassure them that they should be frank and honest in their 360° discussions.

This same HR person may meet this individual on another occasion where their manager is handling a disciplinary matter. Whose side is the HR adviser on? The employee should be afforded all of the protection that the disciplinary procedure and the law allows. Equally, the manager should be given expert advice so that they can handle the matter correctly, but also effectively. If this employee is genuinely not performing to the required standard then something has to be done about it. From the HR adviser's standpoint this is not the easiest of situations to be in. They are meant to be an honest broker but can end up as piggy in the middle.

Just to make the situation even more complicated, if the relationship between manager and employee has broken down the HR adviser has to be careful not to be seen to be taking sides, even if they believe the manager is more at fault than the employee.

Such relationships can be very messy, especially when you introduce union representatives and the manager's boss into the equation. If the HR adviser is not highly skilled they can either be used as a scapegoat or, just as bad, back out of the situation and leave the parties to it.

The only answer to all of the problems we have highlighted which have resulted from a variety of perceptions of HR's role is to work towards a new, commonly agreed role for HR.

A new perception of HR

It is very important to aim for common understanding and agreement as to the required role of HRM. There is no point saying HR should be more proactive if, when they are, senior managers resent their involvement. For example, if the first time the HR manager knocks on the sales director's door to talk about sales trends he is told to keep his nose out of other people's business, HR's role is hardly likely to progress. Even the best operational managers will have to accept that HR can contribute more than just placing recruitment advertising.

HR needs to be in on discussions about strategic direction and long-term planning. The story about the 24-hour banking operation is a good example of this. The design of departments and roles would have to include an HR input, hopefully from an HR person who has more expertise in this area than anyone else in the organisation. Equally, HR should help to shape the processes that the business uses and this will inevitably mean they will need to see as much business performance information as possible.

What they don't teach you at the IPD

So, if this is the new role of the bottom line HR function, and it is a role that requires many additional skills and new expertise, where can the HR professionals acquire such a portfolio? You might think the obvious answer would be the IPD who, after all, are meant to be leading the profession and acting as the custodians of its professional credentials. But, as we saw earlier in Chapter 1, it would appear that the IPD may be run by people who do not even like the term HRM so what chance do we have of getting them to be the source of new HR methodologies, tools and techniques? Very little is the answer. The IPD handles the training needs of new and junior personnel administration staff reasonably well. However, learning how to design an application form is not exactly rocket science.

In my opinion, the things that really matter are not taught at the IPD. Formulating and developing an HR strategy, how to measure the effectiveness of personnel practices in terms of their impact on the business, how to make tight connections between personnel activity and business performance are all the big issues which the IPD has failed to address in terms of offering practical guidance. They do not even give guidance on what works and what does not in personnel practice. They do not seem to know exactly what added value is and how to generate greater value through effective HRM.

Of course if you look at the IPD's 'Directory' of courses and seminars there will be courses which supposedly do address these issues but, if that is what IPD members are learning, why then do they still get such a bad press? It would appear that their training is obviously not impressing the people that matter.

This is not just about courses and programmes though. There is the whole question of capability. To produce a good HR strategy is not easy. It requires someone with a good business brain but an equally good HR brain. Such people are few and far between. So is the profession helping to attract sufficient talent in order for its members to offer this service to the organisations that employ them?

Also, there is the question of entirely new skills and techniques. Accountants are trained to analyse a profit and loss account. Personnel people are trained to analyse jobs. But what techniques exist for analysing the people implications of a profit and loss account – and I do not just mean handling redundancies? Maybe we are really looking at a completely new discipline here which itself requires some fundamental changes in thinking.

But then the IPD does not seem to have a good record of responding to change. It is possible to argue that it has been positively resistant to change – a remarkable situation considering that it is the personnel function that is often tasked with bringing about organisational change.

So, if the IPD does not have answers to the big questions, I am going to do my best to provide some of them myself. The starting point for this is to start measuring the effectiveness of the HR function and the people who work in it.

CHAPTER 5

Measuring and assessing the effectiveness of HR

Are most personnel people unconsciously incompetent?

Why should we start with measurement? Well, there is a well-established model that illustrates just how important measurement is in organisational improvement. It is made up of four stages:

1. *Unconscious incompetence* – i.e. you do not know how bad you are because you do not measure your performance against any standard. So you start measuring and this makes you realise just how bad you are and you achieve a state of …

2. *Conscious incompetence* – a very uncomfortable feeling, the pain barrier you have to get through along the road of continuous improvement. After a time you get much better and you are now in a state of …

3. *Conscious competence* – you have seen the quality improvement teams working and the graphs moving in the right direction. You carry on in this state for a long time until your continuous improvement efforts become so natural that you have finally reached a position where you are no longer conscious of them, you are in a state of …

4. *Unconscious competence* – you have learned so much and you are so good at continuous learning that you can call yourself a learning organisation.

Using this model it is relatively easy to conclude that many HR functions are still unconsciously incompetent because they do not measure properly. The first step towards improvement is to acknowledge this and to make a conscious effort through setting measurable improvement targets.

Many HR teams who have suddenly been asked to measure their effectiveness often start by thinking that as long as they measure something – anything – they will be all right. Unfortunately continuous improvement does not work like that. Measuring the wrong things and things that do not matter are activities that are pointless and ultimately fruitless.

Some of my HR clients decide to gauge their own 'effectiveness' by asking what their customers think of the service they provide. This will tell them something but we must remember that some line managers, who just want a reactive but speedy HR service, will score the HR team against these criteria. My view is that you should not ask internal customers what they think of the service they get until you start offering them a high added value service and they are fully aware of what you are doing.

If HR has to introduce measures they must be the right measures.

The importance of measurement for HR

I often think the best parallel for comparing the HR profession against is the medical profession. Doctors try to look after the health and well-being of the population. Personnel aims to look after the well-being of the organisation's employees. The first thing a doctor does with a patient is diagnose what is ailing them. Once they have found the cause of the illness they can prescribe a remedy. If the patient does not return with the same ailment the doctor assumes the treatment has worked. Health is its own measure of effectiveness.

If we apply this analogy to personnel management then the first step in any human resource issue is to diagnose what the problem is. So is this employee not performing because they are incapable or do they need training? Perhaps they are just lazy or their manager has completely demotivated them by putting them in a job where they are bound to fail? Diagnosing these and more complex human resource matters is a particularly fraught affair. Even if the cause of the problem is correctly identified (a breakdown in the manager/subordinate relationship), there are usually no simple prescriptions that will bring the employee 'back to health'.

Unfortunately, personnel managers do not have the power of doctors. They can often be caught in the middle of situations such as these and throw their hands up in the air to acknowledge that their job is a little bit like marriage guidance counselling. Only the 'combatants' can actually resolve their conflict at the end of the day and usually the objective intermediary, the counsellor, gets no thanks for their pains.

Having been in this situation many times myself I can really sympathise with this view but it does not alter the fact that *either the personnel manager contributes something to this situation or they do not.* There are no marks for effort in industry, and certainly no marks for the wringing of hands. No doubt the personnel manager will talk about 'oiling the wheels' but this is not a very convincing measure of their effectiveness. A more definitive answer is required: has this situation been resolved or not, or will it continue to fester? More importantly, what effect is it having on individual, team and organisational performance?

Lack of measurement or failing to heed what measurement is telling us can be disastrous in the medical profession. We have seen several instances recently, the most notable being the children's heart operation scandal in Bristol in the UK. The death rates from one particular surgery team were much higher than the national average and failure to act on the measures collected resulted in more deaths than these high-risk operations should have caused.

Without good measurement in HR it may not be a matter of life or death but there can be equally disastrous effects on the organisation. Take the growth in the use of competencies as an example. Does this methodology work or not? Has managerial competence improved over the last ten years or not? If you produced figures showing that managers delegate more than they used to, does that prove that this initiative has been effective? For me the only answer that will be really convincing is whether the managers perform better and, as a result, we see improved business performance. Everything else is just hot air.

In Chapter 9 we will look at HRM as the performance management function but for now there is a need to focus just on the subject of measurement, per se. By the way, let us be clear about our terminology. We are interested here in the concept, the principles and the philosophy of measurement. This is entirely different to looking at the practicalities of measuring. *The bottom line HR function has to get to grips with both* but it must understand the principles first. Otherwise it will get bogged down in the very time-consuming and often completely specious activity of measuring anything and everything that moves.

Measurement as a philosophy

It might surprise you if I said that measurement is a relatively new subject in organisational and human resource management, particularly when it is blatantly obvious that organisations have been measuring many things, especially business performance, for years. Indeed, has any organisation ever existed without measurement? Probably not. So how can I say that measurement is still a new subject? Let us look at this question a little bit more closely, by way of an example.

I wonder what the profit margin on a packet of crisps is? After the potatoes, oil, cooking, packaging, distribution, advertising and overhead costs are taken out, how much profit is left? Whoever produced the first packets of crisps, commercially, probably wanted to make as much profit as possible but as there was no competition they may not have had to try too hard. So perhaps they did not negotiate as hard as they could with the potato supplier and perhaps they did not weigh all deliveries of potatoes very accurately. Maybe the number of sacks was close enough rather than actual tons. Let us say these crisps returned a margin of 25 per cent. At the time this could well have been a really attractive margin and the crisp manufacturer was quite happy. Also, as there was no competition, he did not have to worry too much about the future.

Now jump ahead a few decades to a time when there is lots of competition, not only in potato crisps but also from all sorts of competing snack foods. Advertising costs are now an increasing percentage of overall costs and yet it is a very price sensitive marketplace, so margins are much tighter, say down to 10 per cent. Measurement now is much more important. The purchasing team are expected to negotiate the tightest prices they can get. All deliveries of potatoes are now weighed exactly on the weighbridge and the quality team (an added cost) have to ensure that the quality of the potatoes is up to the required standard.

Measurement is not only more important, it has become an imperative and this leads to it becoming a state of mind. A 10 per cent error on weight or quality of potatoes, or any of the other variables, could wipe out a significant part of the margin. Also, the company's management team need to keep their eye on lots of measures, just to make sure they stay in business.

Eventually, we arrive where we are today: a highly sophisticated, highly competitive snack food market with all the big players owned by large, multinational conglomerates. Here the order of the day is share price and shareholder value. Such organisations cannot afford to stand still otherwise they will be snapped up or put out of business. The whole organisation has to focus on every opportunity to add value, even though this challenge is becoming increasingly difficult. This organisation has to ensure maximum quality of supplies and does so by incurring the cost of a quality control team. Everyone is under the microscope and the latest IT systems mean that everything gets measured. To make matters worse, they now sell most of their products through the large and powerful supermarket chains who, in turn, are very focused on their own measurable margins. Greater pressure is being placed on their use of measurement.

Unfortunately, though, the organisation starts to come up against some very unexpected obstacles. In order to drive further improvement they are automatically led to the conclusion that they have to get the best out of all of their people. They want everyone to take an interest in quality so that they can save the cost of a quality assurance team. This means they have to measure how their people are performing and set improvement targets. But this is the least straightforward aspect of measurement. Some people do not want to be measured – it makes them even more accountable and puts them under even greater pressure and leads to stress. The clever ones start 'playing the system' and only work on measures that make them look good. The marketing team produces customer satisfaction surveys that show customers like the product but do not like the price.

Then there is the contentious issue of whether to pay for improved performance. This starts to cause problems because there is a need to separate out the performance of the individual from the team's effort.

The point of this scenario is that, yes, there has always been measurement, but there is measurement and then there is measurement. In the early days, a visual glance at a sack of potatoes was a measurement, of sorts. Grading and assessing the quality of a whole batch of potatoes, using statistical process control, is measurement of a much higher order – in a different league altogether. Those organisations that can produce meaningful employee measures, which directly correlate to shareholder value, will be in the premier division.

Measurement has moved from being a simple check through to more sophistication and has ended up as a complete organisational philosophy. As Robert Galvin (an ex-Chief Executive Officer at Motorola) once said: 'If you don't measure it you're just practising.'

Reasons for measuring in HRM

1. The 'Holy Grail' of linking HR strategy to business strategy can only be effectively achieved through measures. So, if a strategic goal is to improve market share, HRM must immediately start to make connections between its own areas of activity and the goal of market share. No one is saying this is easy. It is probably a great deal more difficult for the HR director to do this than the marketing director.

2. Although the philosophy of total quality management (TQM) and continuous improvement is now seen as a bit 'old hat', a key ingredient of successful total quality systems is having effective measurement systems. This applies as much to HR as any other function. So does the HR team want to continuously improve its recruitment and selection? They cannot do this systematically without appropriate measures in place. We will come later to what qualifies as an appropriate measure.

3. Some might argue that business process re-engineering (BPR) is a management idea that had a very short shelf-life. Certainly, some BPR initiatives got a very bad press. Nevertheless, looking for organisational performance and transformation through a focus on processes is still an obvious area worth considering. HR has two interests here. Business processes have serious people implications as any change in the process changes people's jobs and the training they need.

    Second, HR must constantly look at its own internal processes for improvement. As with most improvement efforts, process improvement demands measurement so here is another reason for HR to measure effectively. In recruitment the time it takes to find a suitable applicant might be of interest but not as interesting as the output of this process, which would have to be measured in terms of the performance of the new recruits.

4. Measurement is also necessary for prioritising. How can the HR function weigh up the relative priorities of different activities and initiatives unless it has good measures in place? There may have to be a choice made between introducing a new reward scheme or a new graduate recruitment scheme. These are very different activities but there needs to be a common measurement system

to decide which is more important, both in terms of organisational value and timing.

5.   The final, and most common, reason for HR teams to suddenly become interested in measurement is the need to demonstrate their worth, which is a more positive way of saying justify their existence. Very rarely do HR teams embrace measurement openly and positively. Measurement means increased levels of personal accountability and there is often a natural reluctance to do it. As we will see later, this is the worst reason for embarking on measurement in HRM.

       Paradoxically, *the bottom line HR function will never have a problem justifying its existence.*

Why there has always been a serious lack of measurement in HRM

HR is well known for its resistance to measurement both in principle and in practice. Consequently there is a distinct lack of measurement. This poses problems for anyone who wants to manage HR in a more systematic way and to seek never-ending improvements.

I shared a conference platform in 1994 with an HR director from a large retail chain in the UK, Boots the Chemist. The subject matter was the use of measurement in HRM. I was the first speaker and covered the subject of what is worth measuring and what is not. My favourite example of a measure that every HR department uses, but which has virtually no use whatsoever, is counting the number of training days per year (that is, the number of people attending training courses multiplied by the days training on each course).

When I had finished, this HR director looked a little sheepish because his first slide had the number of training days that Boots had delivered the previous year. He was slightly apologetic for this figure and suggested that I was right to criticise the measure. However, he excused himself by saying that he was relatively new to HR, having moved from a senior operational role. In his previous, operations role he was used to measuring everything that moved. His basic belief was that he could not do his operational management job without having measures of how the business was doing. He was therefore amazed, when he moved in to head up the personnel function, that they did not seem to measure anything. He saw this as his first task, putting some measures in place to enable him to manage the function. In other words, he was taking the view that he had to measure and he had to start somewhere. It is just a pity that he chose to start there.

While I echoed his sentiments, I think he had made a couple of fatal errors. Measuring business performance, say in cost reduction terms, is one thing but just reading across to personnel and measuring costs is missing the point. Would he have been happier if the cost of training was falling, for example?

His second error was to look just at inputs and not outputs. The number of training days is and always will be, at best, an input measure. There is little point measuring inputs without a corresponding measure of outputs. The only reason why HR people fall into this trap is that input measures are relatively easy to collect.

Not long afterwards, I heard that he had been promoted back into the role of managing director at one of Boots' subsidiaries and you might ask whether his replacement managed to improve on their use of measures. Apparently not. In *Personnel Today*, on 10 October 1995, the new director of personnel was quoted as saying:

> We are not very far down the road of measuring Personnel. There is a danger in saying Personnel is contributing X million to the bottom line, because you can never prove it … We help other

people do their jobs more effectively. Boots the Chemists spends £22 million a year on training. We wouldn't do that if we didn't believe that it works.

Well this must be one of the better examples of stating the obvious that I have seen in HRM. Of course, when HR have just spent £22 m on training they are bound to say it works. They would hardly say they just throw money at training. The only problem is, does it really work and how much longer will boards of directors sanction this level of spend without knowing that it is working? The very fact that *Personnel Today* asked the question about measurement means that it is a subject that refuses to go away, even though the vast majority of personnel people wish it would.

Measuring the 'unmeasurable'

If measurement, per se, has become an important issue, does this automatically mean that HR functions should willingly adopt the philosophy of measurement? In some quarters of the HR world there is still a widely held belief that HR is a field which is not amenable to the normal use of measures. Many practitioners still subscribe to the view that you cannot measure a lot of what they regard as intangibles such as morale, motivation and empowerment. They would argue that HRM is a special case. Some, at the extreme end of this spectrum, would even argue that measurement gets in the way of good personnel practices. They feel that measurement exerts boundaries and limits opportunities for individual development and growth.

This is one of those cases where the same logic can result in two entirely opposite conclusions. I would argue that if HR has to work in an area that is not particularly amenable to measurement, then it is even more reason to try measurement, not less. All the measures used for checking potato deliveries in the crisp company were valid, even though some were more accurate than others. Whatever measures were used, it was unlikely that potato supplies would cause a big problem and, even if they did, it would soon be obvious and something would be done about it. In other words simple measures would generate management action.

In HRM, on the other hand, how do we know whether it is helping the organisation or hindering it? There may be no immediate, obvious signs. If the reward system is out of touch with the market the necessary action may only be taken after many key employees have already left the business, if at all. Even broadbrush staff turnover figures may not pick this up. So not only is measurement crucial in HR, HR has to go to even greater lengths to ensure it has the right measures. However, there are some even more fundamental reasons why HRM should totally embrace measurement and learn to love it.

Meaningful measurement

Once the principle of measurement is established this is not the end of the story. As we have already seen, there is always a tendency to believe that any measures will do. Those who fully embrace measurement will not do a lot of it but what they do measure will be meaningful. So what is a meaningful measure, I hear you ask?

How about this one from Dave Ulrich? In the same 1998 *Harvard Business Review* article referred to in Chapter 1 he says 'HR might inform the line that 82% of employees feel demoralised because of a recent downsizing. That's useful.' Is it? I would have thought it was pretty obvious that most employees would not be over the moon after a recent downsizing. This is not what I mean by meaningful, even if Dave Ulrich does.

The diagram in Figure 5.1 is meant to convey both the strength and meaningfulness of measures. At the left-hand end of the scale HR functions undertake activities with no measurement attached whatsoever. They work on the basis of a complete act of faith. Job evaluation is a good example of this – it is often just assumed that it is the right thing to do.

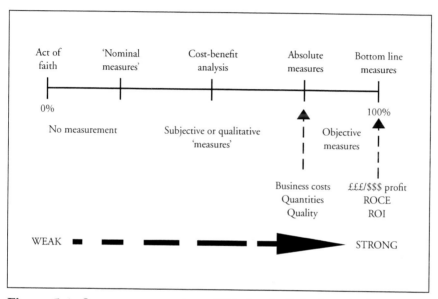

Figure 5.1 Strong measures keep HR closely linked to the business.

In the middle of the scale could be a range of measures that are all subjective, to differing degrees. The results of a staff attitude survey say nothing about staff performance. Nominal measures are those where managers are asked to put a value on various activities, without actually producing real, hard measures. Typically, this happens in training where nominal benefits are attributed to a programme by putting a notional £/$ value on improved customer service.

Cost-benefit analysis can measure costs reasonably accurately but it is usually left floundering when it comes to assessing the benefits of HR activities.

Only at the right-hand end of the scale are the measures really meaningful. Hopefully, training and performance management systems result in improvements in business measures of costs, outputs and quality. The ultimate measure, though, is added value, profit and indicators such as return on investment (ROI) and return on capital employed (ROCE).

In broad terms, the more HR people focus on and use the measures on the right, the stronger the link between their activity and business performance. Again, this represents a fundamental shift in thinking for HR. It has to accept that its activities should have and will have a direct impact on bottom line business performance.

Building output measures into HRM

It is important for HR to focus on the ultimate business outputs of its actions because it completely changes the relationship with the line management. If HR's role is to help the organisation get a better performance from its employees then it should be in a position to discern a link between individual performance and organisational performance.

The real importance of this can be seen during the discussion about filling a sales vacancy between, say, a sales manager and an HR adviser. The bottom line focused HR adviser immediately looks at sales performance as the main business issue and not just how quickly they can fill this particular vacancy. With this mindset they are becoming much more of an accountable partner with the sales manager.

HR people who argue that they cannot guarantee that an employee will perform to the right standard are missing the point. Of course they cannot guarantee it. This is exactly why they need the business measures, because they need to do something if employees do not perform better. The output measures make the HR team much more accountable than basic activity measures such as the time taken to recruit a new employee.

In practical terms, performance will be expressed in such measures as average sales performance in the sales team. Let us say the average sales are £/$100,000 per salesperson per month. The first question is what performance are we expecting from the new recruit? This will lead to a further question about the time it will take the new recruit to get up to speed. Or, alternatively, the sales manager may be interested in an idea to bring a much better sales person into the team to set an example to the lower performers. Interestingly, this sort of discussion would be ruled out of court if the HR team had put in place a rigid pay structure. As always happens, HR has to be viewed in the round and the HR adviser would have to advise on this.

We could develop this scenario further but one thing can be said for certain: the one thing which will keep HR activity very closely aligned with the current and future needs of the business is to constantly focus on what outputs the business is looking for.

The bottom line HR function is a business output focused function.

CHAPTER 6

Benchmarking the HR function

Benchmarking is fine, as long as you know what you're doing

It is probably because measuring HRM effectiveness is difficult that some organisations have chosen, instead, to try to benchmark their HR function against similar functions elsewhere, or even within their own organisation. They believe that this will, at least, give them some basis for meaningful comparison. Also, they hope that if they compare themselves with the best, they may be able to gauge how good they are.

Benchmarking, like any management technique, is only as good as the use you make of it. However, there are several good reasons why we might want to benchmark HR and probably top of the list would be the following:

- Most organisations see the HR function as an overhead and there is only one thing you do with overheads: reduce them. So there will always be pressure to look at the cost and efficiency of the HR function relative to similar functions elsewhere.

- In theory, many organisations seek to gain a competitive advantage by adopting new, innovative HR practices and initiatives, so benchmarking should help to ensure that your own organisation is not left behind by the competition.

- Moreover, benchmarking, as a continuous improvement tool, should also ensure that your HR function will improve continuously and systematically.

So it looks like it might be a worthwhile exercise but where do you start?

Very few, if any, of the proprietary benchmarking systems offered to HR teams to measure themselves actually make any direct connection between HR activity and business performance.

One of the best known and most widely used systems is an American product which employs a 'Scorecard'. This supposedly 'provides hard (numerically quantifiable) measures of people performance within the organization', according to one of their 'Human Asset Effectiveness Reports' that one of my clients showed me in 1999.

This, like many other consultancy products, is a masterpiece of marketing. It offers quantity of data over quality of information. The more measures the better. It is aimed at HR teams who do not really want to be more accountable but instead opt to give an appearance that they are measuring something worthwhile. It is extremely clever because it only tells HR teams what they already know, because it only uses their data. But it feeds back to them all sorts of statistics, graphs and charts which look impressive visually and give an impression that they are able to gauge their performance.

The basic premise on which HR benchmarking is founded is that if you collect the same metrics from different companies in the same or similar sectors and then compare the results across the group, each company can gauge whether they are better or worse than their comparators. This is why benchmarking has earned itself such a bad name. It makes a very simplistic assumption that the best performing companies have the best performing HR teams. Well, Boots was a brilliant performer by the standards of the City but it could well be argued that the HR function was not necessarily a great contributor to this success.

Let us look at just one metric collected by this consultancy: 'average profit per FTE' (full-time equivalent, i.e. an average of the approximate number of full-time employees). You do not need to be a genius to work out that there are numerous variables that would significantly influence this metric and many of them would be outside of the control of the board, never mind the HR function. Take, for example, the cost of computer chips or the price of oil or exchange rates. The price of these can, and has, varied enormously over the last few years. No doubt this benchmarking consultancy would argue that benchmarking with similar companies means such fluctuations have the same impact on each business. If that is their assumption it is much too simplistic. Sourcing oil and chip contracts would vary and companies can take a very different view on hedging against exchange rate variations.

Interestingly, one of their other main 'Key Benchmark Profile' metrics collected is 'training hours per FTE' (a variation on the input measure of training days). It goes further to suggest that: 'Companies aspiring to the epithet – "Learning Organization" – are setting targets of 80 hours training per employee per annum.' Again, the assumption is that this quite arbitrary figure is a worthwhile objective. Yet we all know that this is an input measure not an output measure. As with Boots, it looks like the companies who use such specious data to benchmark themselves have a great deal to learn about measurement. However, it does not stop hard-pressed HR functions using it.

The only thing in favour of this and many similar methodologies is that at least they are trying to bring in a discipline of measurement to HR and all I can say to that is 'amen'. Unfortunately, at the risk of repeating myself, there are never any marks for effort in the cruel world of business and if my criticisms of their methodology are valid (and that is without even trying too hard) then the measures are meaningless. Meaningless measures can be dangerous; they may drive behaviour which is actually not in the company's interest, such as increasing training spend up to 80 hours per person without a corresponding improvement in business performance.

In the UK there is another HR benchmarking consultancy that has built an HR database for comparisons to be made. They, too, seem to think the name of the game is data, data and more data, followed by a spurious analysis and recommendations. The 'Standard Service' offers 'two Benchmarker reports a year with over 200 statistics on the personnel and training function' ('HR Benchmarker', *Personnel Today*, 1 February 2000). Two of these wonderful statistics are ratio of personnel staff to permanent employees (1 : 150) and the time it takes to fill a vacancy (57 days).

What are you supposed to do with this data? Should the ratio of personnel staff be higher or lower? Well surely it depends on what they are doing, doesn't it? In some companies I would agree with Dave Ulrich that they want less of the service their HR team is providing. In others, where the HR function is more closely aligned with real business needs, I would recommend they increase their HR resource.

On the 'time to fill a vacancy' metric, do you want to reduce or increase the time it takes? Well, I would not be too worried for most positions, give or take a few weeks, as long as we recruit the right people. Even if we agree whether the measures should go up or down, there is nothing in these figures that helps us to analyse the causes of the unwanted high or low measures.

You may find it unusual and rather unnecessary to hear direct criticisms of consultancies from someone who makes part of his living out of consultancy work. It could easily be dismissed as professional jealousy or sour grapes. Maybe you are just not used to hearing such outspoken and specific criticism. Perhaps that is because many people do not challenge or work out the failings of such products. Perhaps that is why the HR profession is replete with fads and fashions.

I am quite prepared to challenge anything that I think brings no added value to organisations. Challenging the conventional wisdom and its practices is a key element in organisational learning. It is for this reason that I am prepared to be accused of professional jealousy. Maybe I will have to accept criticism myself in my own personal quest to expose HR practices that just do not work.

Of course you will rarely, if ever, hear damning criticism from the customers of these consultancies. Who is going to admit that, after spending money and a great deal of time collecting their own data, they have learned very little of practical use? The chances are that consultancies like the ones I have mentioned will teach their client companies something, purely by chance, if nothing else. The point is, though, if an HR function wants to take measurement seriously for the reasons outlined above, then they should at least adopt a system that stands up to a reasonable amount of rigorous scrutiny. It should not be this easy to show the fundamental flaws in some proprietary systems. With a good, solid system it would not be that simple.

Effective benchmarking

I have spent the last ten years of my life trying to get HR functions more focused on the same business issues as everyone else in the organisation. Much of this effort has been from the conference platform and, on occasions, it has generated some pretty stiff resistance and even vociferous opposition. But not as often as you might have expected. As someone who is normally introduced as 'outspoken' and 'provocative' I would have expected a stronger reaction more often. This was a conundrum to me for many years, but I now think I know why this is.

The first part of the answer is indifference. Personnel management seems to have been a profession that has attracted some very lacklustre people over the years. They do not get excited or passionate about anything. If I stood on the conference platform stark naked I am not convinced they would bat an eyelid and they would probably be more interested in checking whether I had any spelling mistakes on my overhead slides than they would be in any peculiarities there might be in my physique. There is not much I can do about such people.

By far the biggest group in personnel, though, are those that are convinced, in their own minds, that they are already doing a brilliant job. They have no measures of their own performance but have an unshakeable belief in what they are doing, even if all the evidence points to the contrary. In extreme cases this turns into absolute arrogance where they believe everyone in the organisation cannot see the true value of their work except them, because they operate on a higher plane.

Another trait of such people is that they must be one of the worst groups of copycats in the field of business management. So if big, blue-chip company X is doing 360° appraisal then they must do it as well. This is not benchmarking – this is just replication without questioning anything.

There is nothing wrong with benchmarking, per se. It is a relatively simple technique and many organisations have benefited from using it. But for HR the question is: 'if you walked into another organisation tomorrow and asked to see their HR function would you know whether it was any good or not?' What indicators would you look for? Is there really such a thing as best practice in HR and, if so, what does it look like?

Benchmarking and the myth of HR best practice

Benchmarking best practice is relatively straightforward when used in an operational setting. If you are a logistics director for a drinks company you would probably find some value in benchmarking with a similar logistics operation in, say, a confectionery company. Points of reference might be in average loads, delivery times, fleet costs and the like. All of these are very measurable and improvements in any of them would strongly suggest that the business is gaining value as a result.

The main limitation on benchmarking is that, for obvious reasons, the organisations that you really need to measure your performance against, your direct competitors, will usually be unwilling to share what they have learned. They know it would be like giving away their competitive advantage so they want to keep their 'best practices' to themselves.

While best practice in logistics may be easily discernible, in HR it is a much more problematic concept. What exactly is best practice – the latest fad? The things the best performing companies do or whatever the latest guru says are best practice? Or, perhaps, does *current* practice just become *best* practice when everyone else is doing it? Mike Haffenden, ex-Personnel Director of Hewlett Packard in the UK and a well-known figure in HR circles, has led several forums for leading-edge HR thinking but has come to the conclusion that: 'Best practice does not exist. What suits one organisation does not necessarily suit another' ('Fads and fashions criticised', *Personnel Today*, 5 November 1998).

This view is particularly relevant to HRM where cultural considerations are of paramount importance. So the notion of 'empowerment', for example, cannot be viewed in isolation. It can work in some organisations where the climate is right but would be totally inappropriate where a strong and resistant command and control culture persists. So the HR version of best practice has to be more of a multidimensional concept than in other disciplines.

Now let us look at how HR people use 'best practice' (*sic*) benchmarking. We have already pointed out that the measures they use are rather meaningless (e.g. is 10 per cent staff turnover good or bad?) but what is very intriguing is that HR teams from competing organisations will often openly compare notes on their HR practices. This fascinates me.

If best practice HRM does indeed, by definition, create a business advantage then why would you want to share it with anyone else? Nobody in their right mind would want to do this, unless of course they did not really think it was a competitive issue. Maybe we have something here? Perhaps HR people do not regard what they do as 'competitive'? Instead, perhaps they see themselves as 'professionals' comparing notes to improve their professionalism.

In practical terms, let us look at just one small element of HR activity such as psychometrics. Twenty years ago the use of psychometrics was a relatively new development for most organisations in the area of recruitment. Yet psychometric tests have now become almost a standard tool for selection and assessment as well as initial recruitment. So is using psychometrics best practice or just good practice? Does the use of psychometrics add any value at all?

All of these questions quickly highlight the main issues associated with benchmarking in HR. First, how do we define 'best'? Second, what system should we use to establish who are the best? Maybe if we asked a group of senior HR practitioners to nominate the best would that not be an acceptable and credible benchmark? Unfortunately not, as we will find out later.

Without formal, systematic benchmarking there is a natural inclination to make a simplistic assumption that there must be some causal connection between organisational performance and HR best practice. So, for example, Marks & Spencer had always been regarded as a very successful company so they tended to be recognised as having effective personnel policies. Their personnel policies were also deemed effective because their staff seem to be imbued with the Marks & Spencer culture and appeared to have a genuine desire to give excellent customer service.

So what about another successful corporation, IBM? Sir Len Peach (who used to be IBM's UK Personnel Director, and a previous President of the then Institute of Personnel Management (IPM)) once compared staff turnover rates between IBM and Marks & Spencer during an IPM meeting I attended back in 1987. The IBM figure quoted then was 1.6 per cent per annum, which might, at first sight, appear to be a remarkable achievement, especially if you work in an environment where high staff turnover is the norm (fast food outlets immediately spring to mind).

Staff turnover is often a figure that is used for benchmarking but different levels apply in different industries and under different circumstances. In IBM's case Len Peach intimated that this was an unhealthily low figure. By 1992, when IBM was trying to shed thousands of its employees worldwide, his concerns had proved to be very prescient and one consequence of this low turnover rate was that it cost IBM a fortune in redundancy and outplacement to shed such large numbers of employees quickly.

So, were all of the HR policies that IBM employed, including a no-redundancy policy, best practice or not? Had they been a main contributor to IBM's earlier successes? What can be said, with some certainty, is that, however much they had been successful in the past, they started to look decidedly inappropriate when viewed in the context of their changing fortunes in a rapidly changing world.

This may sound very critical and some could be prompted to defend IBM's policies by suggesting that such criticisms can only be made with the benefit of hindsight. But could we not argue that no company, however successful, can guarantee that it will survive indefinitely or guarantee employment? How can you have an HR strategy that flies in the face of business reality? Could a lack of adherence to basic market principles in its personnel policies be cited as a basis for criticising IBM's former HR practices?

Of even more concern is the thought that if some of the main elements of professional HRM are manpower planning and performance management how can such a large organisation suddenly find itself with so many excess employees? Why had the numbers not been kept in line with market conditions? Bearing in mind that IBM shed its employees, in tranches, on specific dates, it would be ludicrous to argue that up until that time all of these people were usefully employed and that, after that date, their work just disappeared or was absorbed by the remaining workforce.

This is a very serious question as it suggests that HRM was not playing a very important part at all in the way this organisation managed its human resource. It would also be difficult to see how IBM's HR policies had *helped* the organisation to perform efficiently and effectively. The low staff turnover figure could actually be an indicator that many employees must have stayed at IBM precisely because they did not have a particularly difficult or taxing job to do.

If this view sounds a little harsh then we should set it against the following view:

> [IBM employees] had become arrogant, insular and complacent … [Companies like IBM] had been so secure that they had stopped asking their employees to earn promotion, pay rises and job security.

What is really surprising about this quote is that it did not come from the mouth of a critical, external observer like me but from one of IBM's own leadership and management development managers at the IPM national conference in 1993.

Before we leave this subject, one other, very relevant, point is worth noting. IBM was well known and sometimes fêted in HR journals for its 'progressive' no-redundancy policy. Moreover, the company was so wedded to this policy that when redundancies became inevitable IBM could not bring itself to admit it and instead preferred to give the whole exercise titles such as the 'Career Transition Program'! This euphemistic meaningless jargon does nothing to raise the morale of those being made redundant and it failed to mask HR practices that subsequent events revealed to be rather ineffective and misguided.

Why is this point so relevant in terms of HR benchmarking? It is because one of the biggest obstacles to producing meaningful HR benchmarks is that there has to be a clear distinction made between the reality and the hype of HR-driven initiatives – between what is *called* 'progressive' and what constitutes genuine progress. It is the difference between superficiality and substance, sophistication and efficacy. It is the *results* of HRM practices that should be focused on during benchmarking and not the public pronouncements of 'success', where HR specialists are often desperate to justify and validate their actions.

Let us look at another example of an organisation that would appear, on the surface, to be both commercially successful and to have effective HR practices, Motorola. If any HR professional were asked what they thought about HR practices at Motorola, they may well state, if they knew anything at all, that they had heard of Motorola University. The evolution of corporate universities has been capturing the imagination of both business leaders and HR directors (Unipart is probably the best-known UK example) and now there is a definite trend emanating from the USA where many such institutions (virtual or otherwise) are springing up. But do they work and is it a practice that your organisation might like to emulate?

There may well be great benefits to be derived from such an approach to individual and organisational development but how can we be sure? Perhaps the most obvious place to start researching is to look at how such initiatives work out in practice, on the ground.

In this particular case, the head of training at a Motorola manufacturing plant was looking at how effective training and development was in helping Motorola to achieve its business objectives. Motorola, like many other businesses, has a policy that all employees should have at least five days training per year (here we go again with input measures) and we might marvel at this enlightened piece of management thinking.

The more sceptical – dare I say cynical – of us would immediately ask the question, why should there be a minimum or prescribed amount of training for anyone? Is this practice not more akin to the bad old days of sheep-dip training rather than an element of the learning organisation that the scale in Figure 2.1 suggests adds the greatest value? We could also ask those, who focus on training days what constitutes training and does any type of training qualify for this minimum entitlement?

So what can appear enlightened to some can equally appear to be a foolhardy and reckless abdication of management responsibility for training and development.

In this particular instance, the figure of five days of training per employee was actually one of the objectives for the vice-president of manufacturing and it also determined the level of his performance-related pay. In reality, therefore, this target encouraged the number of training days to be achieved rather than training effectiveness. However, this business had serious operational problems and so little training was undertaken for the first nine months of this particular year. Ineffective training, as always, was not seen as a cause of the operational problems. However, in the last quarter of the year, all of a sudden a great deal of effort went into getting everybody on courses before the end of the year. This was regardless of how appropriate the training might have been, but could be seen purely as a means of bringing the average number of training days per person up to five. I wonder why?

As a new HR director looking for best practice, would you follow Motorola's example and set up a corporate university? Would you have a five-day training policy, or not? Benchmarking against a company that has such a policy will bring with it no guarantee of improved performance, especially if the policy is part of a piecemeal approach to HR and there is no focus on business improvement.

If HRM is to remain a credible, professional function there must be some means for answering these questions. It must give the HR director and the rest of the management team a level of confidence that HR is on the right track and performing well, relative to its competitors.

So does benchmarking have anything to offer if what is really needed is a good basis for comparative research? Maybe we need to take a couple of steps back before we try to move forward.

Benchmarking *is* measurement

It is only after producing a benchmarking framework that we can begin to answer, with a sufficient degree of confidence, the questions we have raised about HR effectiveness. Hence the basic need to produce a scale like the one in Figure 2.1.

However, this just provides a starting point. At some stage in the benchmarking process measurements or metrics have to be introduced. Without measurement there is no benchmark. Yet measurement in HR has always been regarded, as we have already seen, as a particularly thorny subject.

In many other functions there are clear and meaningful measures which can be used as benchmarks. In inventory control, for example, probably one of the clearest measures to use would be stock turnaround times. Would there be such a clear metric applicable in HR? We have already looked at the staff turnover rate which can often act as a very rough-and-ready health check for an organisation (assuming it knows what figure is best for its own operations). But linking such a metric to organisational performance is very difficult. Apparently Macdonald's survives very well with a staff turnover of well over 120 per cent.

So, if we accept that we have to have measurements in HR benchmarking, we had better make sure that the metrics we use are meaningful, that is they make a causal link between HR performance and organisational performance. This is where attempts to benchmark HR have often come unstuck.

Linking HR to the business

Linking HR activities and initiatives to organisational performance is extremely difficult. Perhaps a good example to use would be the recent growth in the use of 360° feedback for appraisal systems. In theory, appraisal should be used as a basis for individual performance and development. If it works then effective appraisal should improve organisational performance.

Appraisal is so commonplace now that it is probably regarded as standard practice. So has the popularity of appraisal arisen out of the results it brings or because it appears to offer a relatively simple solution to a difficult problem? Certainly no self-respecting personnel department would be without an appraisal system.

But if appraisal systems have always worked why should there now be a need to move towards 360° appraisal? There are many arguments put forward as to why this more sophisticated approach to appraisal is better, but all we really want is an indication of how it adds value and how much more value it adds than conventional appraisal systems.

Has anyone ever put a value on this particular HR initiative? Actually, a better question is what metrics link appraisal to business performance? Will it reduce costs or improve the quality of the organisation's outputs and, if so, by how much? These are key questions in benchmarking and the same questions apply to HR as much as they do to operational activities.

It has to be said that a great deal of HR activity over the last 20 years or so has paid scant regard to such questions and, all too often, there are very tenuous links made between HR initiatives and real, bottom line business metrics. This may be one explanation for the tendency towards fads, fashions and flavours of the month in HR.

As a basis for research into best practice, HR benchmarking can only be as good as the questions that are asked and the measures that are used. When applied to comparisons of basic personnel administration systems, benchmarking has a very limited use as it is only comparing efficiency. The results of such a benchmarking exercise will probably only help to decide whether to keep these personnel activities in-house or to outsource them.

The true potential of benchmarking HR, however, will only be realised when making comparisons about HR's contribution at a strategic level. Here, questions about the linkages between long-term HR thinking and organisational performance can help, not only to reposition the HR function, but also to provide a basis for a much higher added value role. To make much clearer links between HR and bottom line performance, however, means a new approach, even a new mindset, for many in HR. They have to become more strategic in their thinking.

PART 2

The strategic HR function

CHAPTER 7

When is an HR 'strategy' not an HR strategy?

The difference between business strategy and HR strategy

Of all the management jargon created over the last 50 years the most over-used and abused phrase has to be 'business strategy'. Most people would probably not describe this as a buzzword because its meaning is so obvious and it is now in common business parlance. The reason I am more sceptical about this phrase is that, like buzzwords, strategy is heavy on image and light on substance. The new dot.com companies talk about their 'business models' which are really just forecasts of the number of website hits and customers and sales and advertising revenues. This is probably a more accurate description of what many businesses have and does not really equate to having a clear strategy.

Just because a CEO talks about their strategy does not mean that they actually have anything that could accurately be referred to as a proper strategy. Of course, no one running a large corporation is going to admit that they have not got a strategy because this will make them appear as though they are not in control of their own destiny and will be vulnerable to their more canny and ruthless competitors.

If you had to answer the question 'what is the best business strategy you have ever seen?' I wonder who would be top of your list. I would guess that the number one choice would be the strategy of Jack Welch, of GE fame, who has become a legend in his own lifetime. I do not know who would be in second and third places but how many corporations would be in this league table – 10, 15 or perhaps 20? That is an infinitesimal part of the total business world.

What is it about good business strategies that makes them stand out from the crowd so much? They normally stem from a visionary leader who has crystal-clear thinking, a brilliant business brain and is totally committed to making their chosen strategy work, regardless of how ruthless and brutal that may sometimes appear. They are normally (although not exclusively) long-term thinkers and seem to lead rather than follow the market. There are probably a million other things we could say about the best strategies but most if not all of them would have to be said with the benefit of hindsight. We can only gauge the effectiveness of a strategy by looking at its long-term success.

My own choice for the number one in strategy would have to be Toyota. My workshop and seminar audiences get fed up with me extolling the virtues of Toyota. I wish I believed more companies had equally good strategies, just so that I could give other good examples in support of my arguments. Certainly GE are up there with Toyota but even I was surprised to read in an article in the *Sunday Times* on 31 January 1999 that Eiji Toyoda, 'the genius who built Toyota from a provincial truckmaker into Japan's top motor company' had given advice to Jack Welch. Apparently, after meeting Toyoda, Welch cut a swathe through GE's 'bloated bureaucracy and shopfloor overcapacity' which was a key element in the early days of his attempts to turn GE into one of the most successful companies in the world.

Good strategies, and the strategists behind them, become very much part of our business myths and legends. Brilliant strategies, like talent, are extremely rare, by definition. If talent were commonplace it would not stand out as 'talent'. Because strategic talent is so rare this suggests that formulating and implementing strategies is not easy. More companies get it wrong than right. How do we learn from this though?

Other companies have gone some way to emulating Jack Welch's success, including his own former colleague Larry Bossidy who has achieved similar successes at Allied Signal & Wire. So there are lessons that can be learned and these successes stand out from the crowd. However, can we learn something from companies that have lost their strategic direction?

Here is an interesting story from *The Economist* on 6 March 1999 about Hewlett-Packard (HP):

> Everybody agrees, Hewlett-Packard is a nice company. It has nice, well-engineered products. But it is also just a bit dull. Worse still, there is a suspicion that the celebrated 'HP-way' of doing business may be a little too cosy for it to compete successfully against some of the most relentless firms on the planet. HP desperately needs to inject a little excitement into its stodgy culture and to become, in the words of its gentlemanly chairman, Lew Platt, 'more focused and more nimble'.

As far as I am aware, Lew Platt has been a very successful leader of HP for years with some sparkling results. Yet he is obviously well aware that they need to change. They appointed a new CEO in 1999, Carly Fiorina, to try and bring about some of the necessary changes. I wonder if she can transform HP without being as ruthless as Jack Welch? After all, HP is well known for its progressive 'people' policies and it *is* regarded as a 'nice' company to work for. If HP is to be turned around, will these nice people policies have to go?

You may have noticed that without a new heading or a break in the narrative we have shifted our focus from business strategy to people (or HR) strategy. Whether you have a 'nice people strategy' or a 'hard-nosed people strategy', no CEO can get away from the fact that, if they are going to be successful strategically, they have to have a successful people strategy. Some would say that HR strategy has to follow business strategy. I would go much further and say the two are not separable. As one HR director said to me once 'the business strategy is the HR strategy'.

Another interesting example is Ford. Do they have a good business strategy? It appears from their trail of acquisitions over the last few years that they have a pretty clear business strategy. However, their manufacturing base in Europe is having serious problems trying to make money, especially as it is well recognised that there is significant overcapacity in the European car industry.

There have been several recent announcements from Ford in the UK (at the time of writing in February 2000). First, apparently Ford have decided it would be a good idea to have a scheme whereby all of their employees can have a personal computer at home. Presumably this is something to do with helping their employees to learn new technology and keep abreast of many new developments. Perhaps there is also a belief that a more PC literate workforce will be a more productive workforce.

Second, Ford have just suffered the threat of white-collar strike action, the first for many years, over differentials between white- and blue-collar pay settlements (yes, I too cannot believe that in 2000 I still have to write about 'white' and 'blue' collar workers).

Third, Ford announced that they were to shed about 1,500 jobs at Dagenham. Then there were reports in the papers that there was an atmosphere of resignation about the inevitable demise of the entire Dagenham plant. We now know the plant is to close.

Now, is it just me or do these three different aspects of HRM at Ford not seem to hang together very well? They seem to be rather incongruous and could even be regarded as conflicting. For all I know, there may be a grand design that sits behind all of this but, if there is, then Ford do not seem to have convinced the white-collar staff. Also, how do the production-line workers feel about the new personal computer idea? If workers at Dagenham, or other Ford plants, think their own plant might be on the 'overcapacity hit list' where does the idea of getting a PC off their employer fit in? What is going on in the minds of the striking white-collar workers, who may not even have a job next year?

All of this leads me to just one conclusion: if Ford have a clear and coherent HR strategy they have a funny way of showing it.

Maybe what we are experiencing now is a global business environment where life is just too complex for businesses to have clear, long-term strategies. As soon as you put a strategy into place there are so many variables which cannot be predicted or controlled that the 'best laid plans' can come to nought, or certainly can be seen as seriously off course. This has led some to the conclusion that systematic, strategic thinking is antithetical to the modern business environment. As Lew Platt of HP seems to be suggesting, organisations like his need to be infinitely adaptable to changing circumstances. But that does not stop Lew Platt *wanting* a strategy, or at least *trying* to have one.

Jack Welch is no different. He has to live in the same world as everyone else but his strategic approach has worked very well. GE has faced just as many changes, challenges and complexity as its multitude of competitors but its strategy has seen them through. So anyone who argues that they cannot devise a business strategy is basically making excuses. They are also admitting they do not know where the business is heading. This is not a good state of affairs to be in from the viewpoint of the organisation's employees. If the organisation does not know where it is going neither do they. Forget trying to measure the difference this makes – I think everyone would accept this is not good for business, and neither does it help with morale or employee motivation.

This point is very important for senior HR people. If the basic theory is that business strategy dictates, guides and shapes HR strategy then what can an HR director do if there is no clear business strategy? Just make one up on their own? Or do they do their best to divine where the business is heading?

Or maybe not have an HR strategy at all? In effect, they might have a 'default strategy'. In other words, they react as they see fit. But the term default strategy is an oxymoron. If you are just reacting then, in effect, you have no strategy at all. There are none of the beneficial key components of strategy which are the ability to plan, the ability to communicate a definite direction and the ability to gauge whether you are making progress or not.

The bottom line HR function needs a clear business strategy to be in place. This is a necessary condition but it is not a sufficient condition. Just because the business has a clear business strategy does not mean an effective HR strategy will follow. I think Ford might be a very good example of this.

If good business strategy is rare, and even good business strategies do not guarantee good HR strategies, then good HR strategy must be as rare as hens' teeth. If you follow this logic then maybe we are really getting to the nub of why personnel has such a rotten reputation. But we are also indicating now that this is not really, or at least solely, the fault of the personnel function. They can only work with what they are given and if they are given no business strategy they have to make their own strategy up as they go along. No wonder we have seen so many fads and fashions in personnel management.

Despite this, there is still general agreement among senior HR people that HR strategy is very important. We are back in the world of perceptions as opposed to reality. These same people would argue that they do work to an HR strategy when, in fact, all they have is a series of roughly connected personnel policies, the sort of polices we have already seen being introduced at Ford. Ford knows that their main competitors are doing their best to get the most out of their people. Companies like Toyota (there I go again) have managed to reduce costs significantly, by involving all of their employees in cost-reduction efforts and giving them training to help them to do this. Ford would obviously like to achieve similar cost savings but they will never achieve the same level of savings without a more effective HR strategy.

Car industry observers would probably get annoyed at my, apparently glib, statements and ask me to come up with a way to help Ford. Well, I will certainly try but the first question is why is Ford not already getting good strategic HR advice? Who are the architects of Ford's strategies? Does Ford understand true HR strategy or are their business leaders just trying to run the business the best way they know how? Should they go and have a word with Eiji Toyoda or would they not learn anything?

How about starting with the most contentious strategic HR issue. Should Ford be working with trade unions or not? The answer to this question is very simple – no. How can I be so dogmatic? Quite simple really: *the bottom line HR function should only do things that add value.* The presence of a union does not add value. They more often sap value. If you are going to say some pretty provocative things you might as well go the whole hog.

I have now probably upset many trade union leaders and employers who will argue that their modern, partnership approach to industrial relations means they can work together to get the best out of the workforce. No doubt a partnership with a union is preferable to conflict but why does a company need a union to get the best out its employees? Surely it can do this quite happily on its own?

As a past student of the history of industrial relations and trade unionism, and as a former industrial relations manager, I think I know enough about why workplace industrial relations evolved to where they are today.

Unions did an excellent job of raising employment standards and working conditions and all of us should never forget that. Many employees (not all) still join unions because of a genuine belief that the union will look after their interests. Being a member of a union, in effect, is often an admission by an employee that they do not trust their employer. It has always amazed me that this situation has continued to this day, when this is such an awful basis for what is meant to be a mutually beneficial, productive relationship. It is a situation that many business leaders and HR directors believe they are just stuck with, a case of historical baggage that is not easy to offload. Yet this is exactly the sort of challenge that HR strategy should address because it offers the greatest added value.

For the hard-bitten HR directors who say you cannot get rid of a union I would first ask whether they would be prepared to make removal of the union a long-term strategic objective? In effect, do they have a vision that the company will be able to operate one day, without a union, because their workforce trusts the management to look after their interests? If they do not have such a vision, then the company's default strategy condemns it to many more years of damaging, mutual mistrust. Only when a future, without unionism, becomes a conscious, strategic objective will it start to become a reality. That is why HR strategy is simultaneously so difficult yet offers such high added value.

Such a strategy could be openly discussed with the relevant union officials and employee representatives. This would not be a unilateral strategy but an agreed one. The union would have to be convinced that such a strategy would be in the interests of their members (and probably their own interests). It would require some complete mindset shifts, over a very long period, maybe as long as ten years. Included in the strategy would be the principle of voluntarism – no one would be forced to leave the union. Moreover, there would have to be a workforce representative body established for communication and dialogue purposes (although I am not thinking about the European-style works councils here).

Perhaps the biggest criticism I will have to face for holding this view is that I am naive (or maybe the idealistic HR guy that Geoff Armstrong refers to). The car industry is a tough game by any standards and I have some personal knowledge and experience of this. I know it would be very difficult to introduce a better HR strategy at Ford. It would take many years for a start and maybe they do not see that far ahead. But there is only one reason why I am thinking the unthinkable and speaking the unspeakable and that is I think this HR strategy would add value. I would even go so far as to say that on the day such an agreement were announced to the press there would be an immediate increase in Ford's share price. One thing I know for certain, while Ford is adopting its present 'strategy' it is losing a competitive edge. Imagine all the hours taken up at a senior level within Ford about how to avoid union trouble. All of this is negative energy. Why not put this effort into a positive HR strategy?

Before we move on it might be worth looking briefly at one of Ford's biggest competitors at home (in the USA), General Motors (GM). Do they have a better HR strategy? Well in June 1998 they had a strike costing them $50 m a day. The production workers who were striking were earning $40 an hour. According to *The Economist* (20 June 1998):

> The Flint [Michigan] plant in which some UAW [United Auto Workers union] workers get eight hours pay for 4½ hours work, is particularly inefficient. Even with investment, it would not match Ford's American plants, never mind Toyota's.

No company, starting up today, would want to get themselves into the situation in which GM finds itself and, like all poor industrial relations environments, they exist because that is what history dictated. But that is precisely my point. These are the sort of really big, competitive-edge, strategic HR issues that large corporations fail to address and they pay a very high price for that omission. They may avoid taking risks in this area but they are losing competitive edge every day as a result.

What are the elements of a good HR strategy?

Despite everything said above, the one thing that most, if not all, HR directors would agree with is the need for an HR strategy. They would also agree that it needs to be linked to the business strategy (if there is one) but they would probably have a wide variety of differing views as to what constitutes an HR strategy? So what should the key elements of an HR strategy be?

1. The HR strategy should be formulated as the business strategy is being formulated, not afterwards.

2. There should be a clear statement of purpose for the HR function. Is it a support service or is it an equal business partner?

3. Strategic HR thinking should actually inform the business strategy. The choice of where to get recruits from for the new 24-hour banking operation is a good example of this.

4. An HR strategy is a strategy for organisational change. If the organisation does not need to change then it does not need an HR strategy, as such. Instead it just needs a set of policies (e.g. pay, recruitment and training policies).

5. An HR strategy will, almost by definition, address fundamental structural and process changes. If it does not then a question has to be asked about whether real change is necessary.

6. The HR strategy should be a written document, which shows direct links to strategic business objectives. So, if market share is a strategic objective, the HR strategy should state how it would help to achieve this.

7. HR should be totally accountable. If it says it is going to help achieve an increase in market share then it should share accountability for the achievement of market share targets.

8. A strategy is more than just a plan but the strategy should certainly be set out as a plan with timescales, milestones and targets.

When is an HR 'strategy' not a strategy?

My simplest answer to this question is to use the analogy of an electrician rewiring your house. A good electrician will strip out all of the old wiring, light fittings and sockets and replace them with a completely new system. Shoddy electricians, or those working to a customer's budget which is too tight for the work to be done properly, will just disconnect most of the old wiring and replace it where necessary. However, the most crucial part of the whole job is to make sure the new circuits are all correctly wired into the mains.

Most HR 'strategies' are akin to the shoddy electrician. HR directors do not have either the power or the inclination to do a complete 'rewiring' job. The most damning criticism of such 'strategies', though, is that the HR director usually forgets to wire them into the mains. Or maybe it is more a case of not knowing where the main fusebox is. So, they have some really nice, new, clean fittings but none of them work. In case you missed the subtle point, the 'mains' in this HR analogy is the business plan.

Instead of showing you the connections to the mains, if you ask an HR director what their strategy is they will usually present you with a shiny, new set of policy statements or documents. The pay policy, for example, may state that the company will aim to set its pay levels in the upper quartile of similar companies. It may have a policy on continuous development for all staff and put a personal development review system in place to support this policy.

A good HR strategy will provide a solid foundation on which to build a coherent set of such policies. However, just having a set of policies does not mean there is any semblance of an HR strategy in place.

Is there, for example, a clear statement that underperformance will not be tolerated? Does the company have an intention to reward high performance? Is an upper quartile salary level enough to attract and retain high performers? All of these questions are linked. Without eradicating underperformance, those having to work with the underperformers will have less chance of excelling. If you really want to reward high performers why does the company not want to exceed market salary levels? I would go even further, why cap earnings at all? Or is that too revolutionary for most businesses and their HR experts?

An HR strategy will address all of these questions in the round. It will produce an approach that can address all of these issues simultaneously. The whole strategy will hang together well. So, underperformers will know where they stand and cannot expect a pay rise every year, as a matter of course, to keep up with upper quartile salary levels. The strategy will also have ensured that these messages are communicated well, so that all employees know where they stand.

It is extremely difficult to capture here, on paper, the essence of what makes a good HR strategy. This is just an introduction to the subject and as you read further perhaps, by constantly looking at HR strategy from various perspectives, you will start to gain a much fuller appreciation of what a true HR strategy looks like. It cannot be defined in just a few simple sentences.

What I would say, though, without any shadow of a doubt, is that HR, more than most functions, has adopted a very unstrategic approach to change management. It is often ad hoc and piecemeal and has been driven by all sorts of fads, fashions and, not to put too fine a point on it, completely barmy ideas. Why should this be so? I refer to this tendency as a 'bow and arrow strategy' and it is illustrated in Figure 7.1.

Most operational functions have to focus on the measures set in the business plan. Sales, marketing, production, logistics and even research and development have to deliver to time and cost. It is relatively easy for a logistics director, for example, to get a pretty good idea of how many vehicles and the number of drops per day that are required to meet business plan targets.

The question for the HR director is: 'what is in the business plan which tells me what I have to do in HR?' Well, it might give them a reasonable idea of the numbers of people required and the amount of money available for salaries. If they are lucky, the business plan might even have a certain level of staff turnover included. But that is about it.

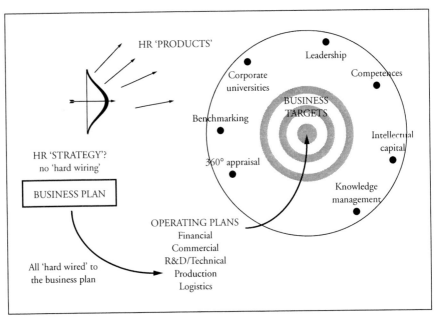

Figure 7.1 The 'bow and arrow' HR strategy.

The business plan says nothing about what training is needed. It says nothing about the types of roles that the organisation needs. It gives no real indication of how flexible the workforce should be to achieve the business targets. It puts no value or targets on ideas, intellectual capital or knowledge. It does not mention the organisation culture and whether it would be a good idea to move from a blame culture to one where employees are allowed, even encouraged, to make mistakes.

All of these are crucial issues but they are very rarely spelled out or made explicit. Yet it is up to the HR director to try and get to grips with such issues because there will probably be a genuine belief, at board level, that these issues must be dealt with if the organisation is to move forward. Let us look at the one issue of 'blame culture' in a little more detail.

You can spot a blame culture a mile away. In a blame culture no one wants to take any personal responsibility for anything. If you are looking for someone to be made accountable you will always be directed to another manager or department. Copious memos (actually, emails these days) will be copied to everyone to make sure that any future blame can be spread or deflected as far as possible. There will be a lack of constructive dialogue between departments and subordinates will be advised to 'cover their backsides' whenever they are working on a project that might go wrong.

Some senior managers have grown up in just such a culture and they learn how to play the game by these rules. They make sure somebody else always makes the final decision or they get their decisions rubber-stamped by the MD first. At least they make the MD aware of what is going on, so that he cannot deny any knowledge of it if it does go wrong. With such managers you cannot be open or honest when you speak to them because you cannot trust them to take it in good faith. Instead, they will see frankness as your weakness to be exploited rather than a virtue to be applauded.

Wise chief executives, who are aware of the damage this does, want to rid their organisation of such politicking and Machiavellian intrigue. So they embark on a programme of open and honest communication. However, they see this as more of an 'HR' issue so they ask the HR director to look after it. So what does the HR director do? Tell the chief executive to get rid of the worst back-stabbers in the organisation? Of course not. Instead, the safer option for them is to make some attempt to develop a more open and honest culture. But this is a no-win situation. Once the back-stabbers get wind of what is happening they are cunning enough to mount their own campaign to hold onto their hard-won positions of power.

Rather than confront this problem head on, it is much easier for the HR director to opt for a solution that *looks* like it is dealing with the problem, even though it is just window dressing. So they bring in a consultant who introduces the idea of 360° feedback, a system which allows subordinates and colleagues to air their views about these managers. The aim is that, once the back-stabbers have been made aware of their dastardly behaviour, they will start to change. And pigs might fly.

Such initiatives have no clear objectives set. There is no direct link made between the 360° initiative and business objectives (will a more open culture reduce project costs and times?) and no one, therefore, will ever be able to say that the 360° initiative succeeded or failed. In the meantime, however, the HR director can report to the CEO that work on the 'culture change' is well underway. More importantly, they can measure the number of managers who have been through the 360° programme (a great activity measure). The HR director then hopes that, before the CEO is ready to ask any serious questions about progress, his attentions have turned elsewhere.

So Figure 7.1 shows how the politically astute, yet personally unaccountable, HR director's 'strategy' is one of firing off different initiatives (arrows) in all directions hoping that this range of activities will take the heat off himself (I am tempted to say 'or herself' but I have to admit that this sort of behaviour manifests itself much more in men than it does in women, in my experience).

Another HR director may have a different modus operandi. While not particularly under pressure they may read all the latest management journals and want to make a great show of their efforts to help the business. So they try out all the same fads and fashions, hoping that some will actually hit the target. But they are not inclined to be more specific about what these initiatives are attempting to achieve and certainly do not want to measure any outcomes.

These may be extreme examples but they are both different versions of bow and arrow strategies and, regardless of the reasons behind them, they are destined to be equally ineffective. But then that is usually what they are designed to be anyway.

So what exactly should an HR strategy look like?

Let us take a look at a chocolate manufacturer. This company is under pressure because its share price is slipping. It is in a very competitive environment (fast moving consumer goods) and its performance of late is regarded by the City as being stodgy, to say the least. So at a board meeting the directors sit down to discuss the future.

At this meeting the marketing director throws an idea onto the table that the company has brilliant brands and ought to diversify into other products but launch them with existing brand names. So their popular chocolate bars can be developed into a new type of chocolate ice cream bar (yes, I am thinking of one particular company).

A hush settles around the boardroom table as this simple idea filters through and gradually it looks like this one might actually fly. Figure 7.2 tries to represent all the hoops that this idea has to jump through on its way to becoming a reality.

In the first hoop the questions of why have a new business strategy and what products to introduce are being discussed. This narrows down to a more detailed discussion of the markets the company wants to enter. So will these ice cream bars be sold in small retail outlets, through big supermarkets or even from traditional ice cream vans?

Also, how expensive will they be and which socio-economic group are they aimed at?

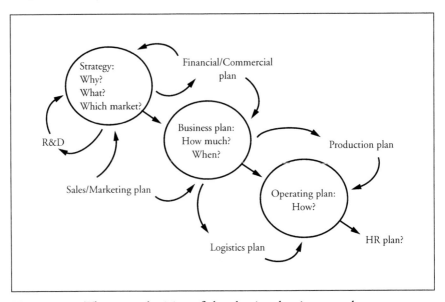

Figure 7.2 The complexities of developing business and HR strategies.

It is not long before the CEO wants to get some financial projections of costs and potential sales. Only when this information is available will the right decisions be made. Of course, this whole discussion does not just follow a simple course. Most strategic discussions are dynamic. You can come up with an idea first or already have identified an existing market to attack. Strategic discussions are replete with different scenarios based on completely different assumptions and changing variables.

So the R&D team are tasked with producing some prototype bars and marketing are asked to market test them. All of this requires funding and the resources have to come from somewhere so the discussions now include making provisions in the business plan. It is getting one big step nearer to becoming a reality.

At some later stage it moves down into looking at operational issues. What do the production team need to produce these bars. How much new equipment will be needed? Logistics jump in and say that they will, of course, require refrigerated transport for ice cream and, as the sales projections start to firm up, the sales and distribution teams work on sales and distribution channels and deliveries.

When all this work has been done, and most of the decisions made, a plan is produced. This plan shows how many new production workers are required, how the existing salesforce will sell the ice cream bars and retraining plans will be drawn up for lorry drivers who need to understand the difficulties of delivering a product which has a tendency to melt very quickly.

The big question, in terms of HR strategy, though, is 'has a strategic HR view been taken, when was it taken and how did it contribute to the discussion?' Were the HR issues uppermost in the minds of those around the boardroom table from the start? The first strategic HR questions tend not to be focused on operational matters. So, perhaps the HR director should ask whether the last big product launch was a success and, if not, what lessons had the organisation learnt? Are there blockages in the company that seem to stand in the way of innovation?

We have already touched on the union issue. Rather than asking 'how will the unions react?' the bigger question that should have been asked at some stage is 'wouldn't the company be better off working without a union?' I refer to this particular issue again just to distinguish between operational HR issues and truly strategic questions.

Regardless, though, of the bigger picture and some of the cultural and structural questions, at some point the discussion will become entirely operational in focus. So, has someone decided whether to use the existing salesforce or a new, separate salesforce? If ice cream bars are to be run as a separate operation what are the structural and process implications of this (and the egotistical issues surrounding who gets the big job)?

If salespeople can visit existing customers to sell ice cream as well as chocolate bars, will average sales per person rise significantly? How about recruitment? Should the company aim to poach some existing ice cream salespeople from their competitors? What effect will this have on pay levels for the salesforce and internal comparisons and relativities?

What effect will refrigerated distribution have? Will there be separate warehouses and who will operate them? Should the organisation recruit someone from a similar operation where refrigeration is a particularly big issue? As this is a key strategic aim, would it be worth offering a particularly attractive package to attract the best calibre of person to look after this side of the business, at least during the transition phase? How about offering a short-term contract because, once it is up and running, there will be a very different requirement for the day-to-day operation of the refrigeration warehouse?

For every strategic business decision there are a multitude of HR issues and *anticipating* them to produce a coherent strategy is no mean feat. It requires a great deal of experience of working in large organisations and understanding the stresses and strains that such fundamental shifts in business strategy place on an organisation.

Admittedly, many businesses going through such fundamental change somehow manage to cope and achieve their strategic goals but that is not the same as saying they have done so as smoothly as they could have. HR strategy is a means of achieving strategic objectives but it also aims to make any organisational transition that is necessary as smooth as possible. The changes should reap the greatest rewards for the business with the least disruption for the workforce.

The overall aim of a strategic, bottom line HR function is to produce a totally integrated, coherent and measurable strategy. In addition, there should be some means of checking whether the strategy is working and, if it is not working, a way of identifying where it is falling short or going off course. However, there are often some big obstacles that get in the way of producing such a strategy. Indeed, effective HR strategies are rare because these obstacles often prove insurmountable.

The strategic dilemmas

I call these obstacles to producing effective HR strategies the 'strategic dilemmas' because they are all double-edged swords. They may not be easy to deal with but if you know what to look for then at least you have a fighting chance of overcoming them.

Principles, values and strategy

First on the list is the idea of honesty. Is it idealistic to expect business leaders to be completely honest? Possibly. What CEO wants to tie their colours to any particular mast when they may be hoist by their own petard at a later date, if that is not a mixture of metaphors? There is always a temptation for a CEO to make public pronouncements that impress the financial analysts in the City. So we hear more and more about claims that a particular CEO is going to double shareholder value in three years, or something along similar lines.

Unilever are currently pursuing a business strategy of reducing their number of product lines from approximately 1,500 to 400. They want to focus on the products that return the most value. As a consequence of this strategy the people working in each division have been told quite clearly that if they do not achieve their targets then Unilever will divest itself of their part of the organisation.

Here, a clear business strategy starts to have an immediately discernible impact on everyone who works at Unilever. The best strategists seem to do this. They tell their workforce what is expected and what will happen if they do not make the grade. Is this hard-nosed or just straightforward honesty and highly effective management?

Regardless of the reasons for it, there will never be an effective HR strategy if the business does not have clear values (e.g. the shareholder comes first) and principles (e.g. personal accountability). The HR director at Unilever has something very focused and tangible to work to. Consequently, they should have no excuse for not producing an effective HR strategy.

Unfortunately, even in businesses that set themselves some tough targets, they are often reluctant to get this message across clearly to their employees (perhaps HP are in danger of doing this) because it might signify a different management style which their employees are not used to. The bottom line HR function, therefore, has a key role to play in prescribing some strong medicine. If it shies away from this task it will slip back into its former, faddish behaviour where it never gets to grips with the real issues that the business has to face up to.

Short term versus long term – the biggest red herring?

Perhaps one of the biggest red herrings in strategic HR thinking is that HR strategy is inherently long term, while there is always a tendency, particularly in western economies, for business leaders to engage only in short-termist thinking. In other words, HR and business strategies work to different and irreconcilable time frames. This is a brilliant excuse for not producing any meaningful strategy and is actually totally fallacious.

There is no reason why short-term needs and long-term strategy cannot be accommodated simultaneously, and even if HR strategy tends to look at the long-term it still has to incorporate ways of managing day-to-day immediate issues. Take, for example, the need to reduce costs on a daily basis. One very short-term approach to this is to just dictate to all managers that they have to reduce costs in their own area by 10 per cent. Very little thought may have gone into this dictat but it will, no doubt, result in some cost reductions, even if, on occasions, the cost reductions are made at the expense of some longer-term need. So, product development costs are reduced but, in the long term, this results in less new products being brought to market. This means, ironically, that the initial cost-cutting decision, which was most probably taken in a vain attempt to improve value, actually results in the organisation losing value.

So where does a longer-term HR strategy fit with this short-termist, short-sighted view? First we need to move away from the traditional management approach of asking all managers to reduce their budgets by a uniform amount. This initiative needs to be selective. Then, how about a very short programme, for the managers selected, to ensure they only cut costs that will generate genuine savings, without longer-term damage being caused? But, at the same time, a longer term management development plan can be put in place to ensure that, the next time cost savings are required, these managers will already be well prepared and will even have been reducing costs on a regular basis anyway.

A few years ago a director of a large car spares business in the UK informed me that Toyota (I'm at it again) had embarked on a cost reduction programme which aimed to reduce its cost base by 50 per cent over three years (yes, I was speechless as well, especially as I already regarded them as super-efficient). At the time, they were already 18 months into this programme and apparently they were on target. The only way they could ever have achieved this was by developing their employees' cost-reducing skills over a very long period. This was no surprise though. Their business-focused HR strategy requires that all employees should constantly be thinking of ways to reduce costs. They recruit people who are willing to accept this condition of employment and then they give them training to help them to do so.

Those who say HRM is hampered by short-termism would argue, no doubt, that this is the main reason there is very little evidence of effective HR strategies. Any distinction between short and long term though is specious. I am an economist, so I know only too well that today's short term accumulates to become tomorrow's long term. It is a pity that this confused thinking results in short-term solutions being chosen to the detriment of long-term development. It does not have to be this way.

Surely the aim of HR is to find a strategy that gets the best of both worlds, some short-term quick wins and longer-term progress and development. *However, HR should never attempt to have a long-term HR strategy if there is no long-term business strategy*, not unless the HR director really feels he or she can start to actually inform and influence business strategy.

If Ford used short-term tactics in HR 20 years ago they are reaping the consequences of that thinking today. Consequently, they may well still be acting short-term because they have never addressed the underlying, fundamental, strategic issues. It sounds like a recipe for a vicious circle.

I am sorry to bring up unions again but their continued existence is good evidence of a lack of both long-term, strategic HR vision and strong HR functions. However, I could just as equally cite a failure to make performance related pay work and an inability to take training and development seriously as examples of short-termist HR thinking.

Reactive versus proactive

One debate that has raged in HR circles for many years is the old chestnut of whether HR is reactive or proactive. HR strategy, by definition, has to be proactive. It has to be based on a vision of the future. It has to anticipate and plan ahead. There will always be a certain amount of reactivity in day-to-day personnel work – maybe a sudden increase in demand, a competitor makes an announcement that seriously affects your business or the government decides to change its policy. However, the best strategists will either already be ahead of the game or will have a certain amount of contingency or flexibility built into their own strategies.

Refer back to the scale in Figure 2.1 for a moment. It is worth noting that a shift along the scale from left to right is also a shift from reactivity to proactivity. The reactive personnel administration team will fill a vacancy as soon as they can but the strategic HR team will help to make the decision that the vacancy exists in the first place, as far in advance of the need as possible.

'Command and control' versus freedom to act and empowerment

One of the most difficult issues for older managers (if there are any left) to face up to is the debate about how much control they should exert as opposed to allowing people the freedom to think for themselves and make their own decisions. This dilemma was very perceptively summed up by Niall Fitzgerald, Chairman of Unilever, in an interview in *The Times* on 18 September 1999:

> We're going to have to find ways in which we can run our business [yet] give much more freedom and control to the

individuals who are in the business ... We're not going to mandate ... the day-to-day how you do it but there are a set of principles by which you will do it which you must never depart from, because that's the soul of our business.

This thinking leads him to conclude that Unilever has to accept a

much more fluid environment in which we have to operate [while] looser arrangements between people internally and externally puts an ever greater premium on the clarity of articulation from the top with regard to what business is about and where it's going. If those are not expressed in a tight, clear, consistent way the thing will just break down in anarchy.

Command and control style cultures did not require brilliant, creative, innovative HR strategies. The management style in such organisations was 'like it or lump it'. They made all the decisions and then informed their staff as and when they saw fit to do so. Niall Fitzgerald is now saying that this type of management style is totally unsuited to the challenges that large, modern organisations face.

I am sure Unilever were always interested in clear, strategic business thinking and planning and he is not moving away from this basic concept. Nevertheless, his statements are a very clear admission that incorporated into the business strategy must be a crucial element of HR strategy. Interestingly, one of the most important elements he refers to is 'clarity of articulation'. Sending 'tight, clear' signals to the workforce is of paramount importance. We covered this under the first strategic dilemma and this just illustrates the many-faceted, holistic and integrated nature of effective HR strategy.

Managing complexity

The final strategic HR dilemma is that of managing complexity. No one would deny that running any sizeable organisation today is anything other than a very complex affair. Relentless competitive pressures, globalisation, the spread of e-commerce, increasing legislation, technological change and a whole host of other variables makes for a very complex mix of factors which have to be considered, balanced and acted upon.

Complexity and the speed of change do not seem to lend themselves to long-term strategic thinking. How can boards of directors manage and control something that is subject to such a wide variety of different forces, many of which are, actually, totally outside of their control? Some argue that in such circumstances it is impossible to work on the basis of well-formulated, clearly defined strategies.

Complexity is a serious issue and appears to militate against organisational strategy. I was lecturing a few years ago, to a group of very senior people from various departments of the Ministry of Defence and the armed services in the UK, who had a specific responsibility for personnel. They said that they all faced numerous constraints on their freedom to make strategic decisions. They had to skilfully persuade, manage and convince a wide variety of stakeholders – their top brass, the government, other civil servants, pressure groups, NATO, the UN, uncle Tom Cobbley and all. As a result of all of this, they argued, they could not predict the future with very much certainty. Consequently, it undermined any explicit attempt to devise a coherent organisational strategy, never mind HR strategy. In other words, complexity and strategy are not happy bedfellows.

From the same premise I would argue the opposite. *It is* precisely *because we cannot predict the future, with absolute certainty, that we need a strategy.* A total lack of strategy means being totally reactive. This is a very vulnerable state to be in. It is the description of a victim of circumstance. When I played devil's advocate with this group and levelled this accusation at them it was interesting to see their response. 'Uncomfortable' does not really begin to describe it. You see, if you take away someone's excuse that they cannot have a strategy, you put them fairly and squarely in a renewed state of accountability.

You are either strategic or you are not, although some try to obfuscate the whole issue by talking about their 'default strategy'. This is sophistry. If the word strategy means anything it includes planning and having some clearly defined strategic goals. You cannot have a 'reactive', ad hoc strategy. That is a contradiction in terms. This is true of organisational strategy but it is even more important for HR strategy.

The HR myths

Another debate in HR that has been around for a very long time is whether HR can have an influence at strategic levels. The extent to which HR is allowed or encouraged to develop a proper strategy will be dictated, as we have already seen in Chapter 1, by its position and credibility in the organisation. However, saying you have an HR strategy is one thing but is it really a strategy in the sense that it is closely linked to the business strategy? Also, is it a clear indication of HR's influence at a strategic level?

Someone who has looked at these questions very closely throughout his career is David Hussey. In his book *Business Driven HRM*[1] he is very honest when he refers back to his earliest attempts to link HR to the business, concluding that he

> believed strongly in the strategic link and was convinced that closeness to strategy was enough to achieve this. We did audit

our HR activity, but this was against a concept of what was good practice, rather than against the specific needs of the organisation. If asked at the time, I would have claimed that the personnel activity was business driven … My answer would have been wrong.

I take my hat off to David Hussey. How often, in the world of modern management texts, do we hear authors admitting they they had got it wrong? Yet it is exactly this admission that gives us very valuable insights into how HR can become more effective.

Compare his views to Ward Griffiths who, at the time of writing, is the Assistant Director-General at the IPD. He was writing in *Personnel Today* (1 February 2000) in the face of mounting criticism that the IPD was not helping to achieve HR influence at the highest levels. Several surveys, including one from Cranfield University in the UK, had shown that HR was losing its seat at the boardroom table and was therefore losing its ability to influence strategy. On the specific issue of HR representation on the board he wrote:

> The issue of boardroom representation for HR is often regarded within the function itself as a red herring … Board membership itself does not equate to influence. Non-membership does not mean the personnel director has no influence on strategy.

To try and make a virtue out of HR not being represented at board level is slightly disingenuous, to say the least. I agree that the fact that an HR director sits on the board is not a sufficient condition for an organisation to have an HR strategy, but it most definitely is a necessary condition. To suggest otherwise is either naive or just flannel to justify, in my opinion, the IPD's own lack of strategic influence.

Let us return to what seems to me the more honest view of the world held by David Hussey. He has addressed this issue much more succinctly than most and cuts through all the rhetoric with his eight 'HR myths'. 'Myths' is a great choice of words because many HR people have been using these supposed truisms as excuses for far too long. Hussey shatters them all.

1. If the top HR manager is on the board this is enough to ensure that HRM is business driven.

2. If HRM is allowed to be proactive when new corporate strategies are considered this automatically means that all HRM activities will become business driven.

3. Doing things right automatically means that we are doing the right things: therefore it is enough to apply good professional practice.

4. Because new HR policies and procedures take a lot of time and effort to implement, they will have a long shelf-life.

5. Evaluation and performance measures are too difficult and expensive for HRM activities, and HRM does not need to be subject to such disciplines.

6. In any case it is not possible to evaluate the results of many HRM actions which should be treated as acts of faith.

7. Every action we take in HRM is with a concern for the interests of the organisation, which means that we are business driven.

8. Line management knows that HRM is a valuable, value adding strategic partner which plays an irreplaceable role in the management of the organisation.

From Hussey (1996).

A simple model of strategic HRM

We looked at a simple model of personnel management in Chapter 1. This was almost a two-dimensional model based on a very simple relationship between the line and personnel, where there is very limited scope for change.

We now need to look at a model for strategic HRM. This has to be multidimensional and it has to have a mandate from the board to act as an agent of change. It is represented in Figure 7.3.

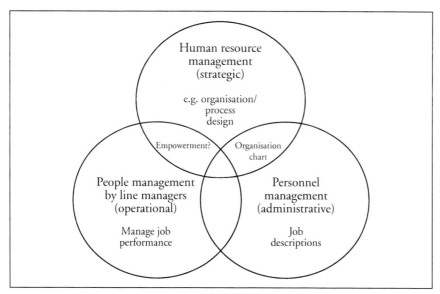

Figure 7.3 A simple model of strategic HRM.

In the simple personnel management model in Figure 1.1 on p. 12 the organisation chart was decided by someone other than the head of personnel or any line managers. They had no say in the matter – it was a given as far as their freedom to make decisions was concerned. However, in the strategic HR model in Figure 7.3 there are no such parameters or scared cows. Everything is open to question – the status quo can and should be challenged by the head of HR if they believe it to be in the best interests of the organisation.

The model allows the senior HR team to have a direct input into designing the structure and processes best suited to the needs of the organisation. This could mean having a very flat management structure with shallow reporting lines. In such a structure the notion of empowerment is important. Without many layers of management to act as the checks and balances in decision-making, employees lower down the pecking order are expected – even empowered – to make their own decisions. So the customer services technician, the chargehand, the staff nurse, the policeman on the beat are allowed to make more of their own decisions on the spot, without reference back to a higher authority.

There is still an important personnel administration need for a job description and person specification to be drawn up for recruiting or selecting such people, but the type of person chosen and the skills and personality sought are now very different from the previous strict command and control structure and culture.

In the line manager's circle their role has changed significantly. Their management of performance is now much more 'hands-off' than hands-on. They may have a bigger team who only seek advice and guidance when they really need it. Indeed, they may only see each other as a team on fairly infrequent occasions.

All three circles overlap and, if I could draw all the dimensions on paper, a picture would emerge which truly represents the interrelationships. The HR director has already convinced the operations director that this new structure will work but they will also have made sure the operations director wants to make it work and does not fight against it. They will also have ensured that support is given to line managers trying to manage in a different way.

There may well have been a large communication initiative to introduce these changes with management briefings, roadshows and the like. Pay, recognition and reward systems will have been designed to ensure that the most effective types of behaviour are encouraged rather than discouraged. Those who will not make it through the transition period will already be on a programme of redundancy, outplacement or career counselling.

All of this will happen in such a way that the organisation moves forward and progresses rather than suffers the pain of change without making progress – but only if the HR strategy is right and implemented effectively. The HR strategy sits on top of many operational as well as purely personnel issues. It provides the coherency that change management requires. It ensures there is a 'clarity of articulation' throughout the whole process, as Niall Fitzgerald might put it.

Linking HR strategy to business strategy – a framework

Most of what has been said so far, hopefully, makes sense. If it does not then thanks anyway for reading this far. If you are still on board with the basic ideas then we now need to look at turning strategic HR thinking into a workable reality.

Of course, every organisation will have to put together its own HR strategy and they will all be unique (although, as we have seen, HR's obsession with copying 'best practice' has resulted in most large blue-chip organisations actually having exactly the same HR policies). Nevertheless, the framework offered here gives some simple guidelines which are intended to ensure that the HR strategy is not only devolved from the business strategy but is also clearly linked to measurable, strategic objectives and actually starts to inform future business strategy.

Checking strategic thinking

Before even considering HR strategy we need to know how well-developed strategic thinking is already.

Vision

Does the CEO have a vision of the future? How far into the future do they look? Let us look at a hospital as an example. I wonder what the hospitals of the year 2020 will look like? Will they be funded out of taxation or will they be run on quasi-commercial lines? Will technology replace much of the labour-intensive side of the health service? Perhaps many of the diseases we have today will have been eradicated but then again maybe they will have been replaced by much worse.

All of these are very serious questions but they cannot be answered, with much certainty, very far in advance. Nevertheless, a good leader will have their own vision of what the future holds and will start to guide their organisation towards that vision. Vision is at the pinnacle of strategic thinking. Everything should follow on from this vision. This is what the diagram in Figure 7.4 suggests.

Without a vision of the future how can a CEO know what the organisation is going to require in the long term? More importantly, if you work in an organisation that has no vision how do you feel about that? It is not the best way of motivating staff, is it, to admit that you don't know where the business is going. It hardly gives employees that nice feeling of security that so many crave.

However, while vision can be incredibly important, it is conspicuous by its absence in most organisations I have ever worked with. Moreover, visionaries' predictions of the future are probably wrong just as often as they are right. Bill Gates, of Microsoft fame, had the right vision to realise that a good operating system could achieve a monopoly. However, he had no vision that the Internet was going to be as big as it is.

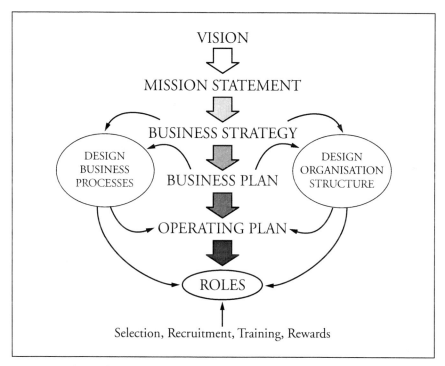

Figure 7.4 Linking HR strategy to business strategy.

The real question, though, is how can an HR director have an HR vision if the business leader does not have a business vision? Even if there is a business vision, is there something tangible in this vision that allows HR to start to develop its own vision?

Somebody once told me that a car company had a 250-year vision. It just said that it would be making modes of personal transport in 250 years' time. We could now discuss whether this was a good vision or not, but that would be missing the point. Business is inherently risky and vision is difficult to criticise by any other means than with the benefit of 20 : 20 hindsight. The real question is how do you start to make the vision a reality? If you were the HR director at this car company it does very little to guide your thinking and actions except to give you a great deal of confidence that you can plan long term. It also sends some pretty clear signals to the workforce that this business is committed to a long-term future – a very powerful and motivating message.

So, although the theory of strategic thinking is actually pretty simple in essence, it rarely works so smoothly in practice. One academic definition of vision is that it has no measures attached – it just sets a general course. Vision offers nothing tangible for HR to hang its strategy on. To get the best, tightest links HR needs something more tangible than that to focus on. So, instead of focusing on vision, HR should be linking its own strategy to something more meaningful. The next possible port of call is the mission statement.

Mission

The actual terminology is not too important here. Different organisations seem to use vision and mission interchangeably. I always refer to missions and mission statements as the second level of strategic decision-making but I often see 'vision statements' used in the same way.

Unfortunately mission statements have become a very tired cliché. Like all clichés the original power and meaning of the word has been lost. Some years ago, during the total quality revolution, every self-respecting CEO had to have a mission statement. Usually it resulted in some anodyne, meaningless claptrap that did nothing to inspire or motivate the workforce. As such they were often derided and quietly forgotten about.

This is a real pity. Like all good ideas, mission statements ought to be resurrected because they can be incredibly powerful and galvanise organisations. Canon's 'beat Xerox' has to be one of the best mission statements ever. It was so focused. When I worked with some people at Canon I asked them about this legendary statement and one guy just smiled and said, 'yes, we did that some years ago'. They had now moved on.

Let us stick to the object of this exercise though. Can HR link its strategy to a mission statement? If the mission statement says 'beat competitor X', is that a solid foundation on which to build an HR strategy? Well, it is certainly more meaningful than a broad vision. Ideas that would immediately run through my 'HR brain' include attracting better people than Xerox, or perhaps poaching some of their people. We could look at their product development lead times and aim to beat them. This may lead to a review and restructuring of our own product development process. So a good mission statement does at least start to point us in the right direction in terms of HR strategy. But it would be very dangerous to try and build a complete HR strategy on the basis of this alone. We need something even more tangible, more measurable.

Strategy

So perhaps the next level down will help: the actual business strategy document, assuming there is such a thing. Actually, there are many reasons why we do not see strategies set out as clearly and succinctly as we would like, in a single document:

- Maybe the CEO and board do not have a clear strategy.
- Even if they did, producing such a document leaves them open to criticism if they do not achieve it.

- Who wants to run the risk of providing a competitor with a complete overview of their strategic plans?

- Writing strategies down is actually quite difficult (you may have already noticed).

So, looking at the business strategy is not such a straightforward exercise. The few things that tend to be included in strategic documents, though, are some numbers and timeframes. These may not be set in stone but they start to put more flesh on the bare bones of a mission statement. In the ice cream bar example above, the strategy would indicate which markets are to be attacked first – the UK, Europe or America? Overall sales volumes may also be stated and deadlines set.

Even at the business strategy level, though, while a full understanding of the business strategy is crucial for the senior HR team, it does not give them enough detail to work on. Only the business plan will start to provide this.

Business plan

My simple definition of a 'business plan' is that it will look further forward than one year and will have profit and loss and budgetary figures in some detail. Usually, it will have a three- or five-year time horizon. It may actually be a 'rolling plan' which changes every year, but the figures will always be adjusted accordingly. By looking at the measures in the business plan the intangible vision, mission and strategy become tangible.

The business plan is the first point at which the architects of the business plan become accountable. The CEO and all other senior managers should be judged against the business plan at the end of each year. The business plan not only provides an excellent basis for developing a practical HR strategy, it also provides a high level of confidence that the senior management will own and support the HR strategy.

As an example, if the business plan says sales of ice cream bars will go from zero to £10 m in one year and the HR team develop training and pay systems to support this, both the sales director and the HR director should be working hand-in-hand towards a common goal. HR strategy will not be a detached, ivory tower exercise.

We must not lose sight of the fact, though, that this business plan should have been born out of a clear and coherent vision, mission and strategy for the whole framework to work best. If these other levels are not working well then the potential benefits of HR strategy are bound to be limited. At least the HR team can be confident, though, that by focusing on the business plan they are still closely in touch with current management thinking.

Operating plan

However, this is not the end of the story. One thing we can say with absolute certainty is that every organisation has a one-year operating plan (or at least a budget) to work to. So, while HR is thinking long term, it has to ensure that its HR strategy also deals with the here and now. If it was not given much notice then it will have to make sure the requisite number of ice cream salespeople are in place and check that initial sales targets are being achieved.

Whenever I meet an organisation for the first time I always use this framework to check how much is in place and what gaps there are. It does not take too long to find out how far into the future the organisation is looking, especially if the only business plan is a rolling, one-year plan. Simple questions to the board such as 'so what do you think the market will look like in five years' time?' are very quick indicators of the existence or non-existence of any visionary leadership.

What I am looking for in a perfect world (yes, I know nobody's world is perfect) is a well thought-out, long-term strategy based on a clear vision. Each level of strategic thinking should dovetail together. More often than not I am disappointed but I never give up using this conceptual framework because the very least it will do is highlight some serious organisational weaknesses. This, in itself, is very fertile ground on which to develop a high added value HR strategy. In fact, if the business is that bad at running itself, strategically, then effective, strategic, bottom line HR people should be able to say 'move over and let me show you how to do it.'

I was asked to tender for some work quite recently for a local government body. The brief was to help them decide what their strategic objectives were and to identify key performance indicators which could be articulated to the rest of the organisation. I have to say that if the board needs help with this fundamental part of their job then they must have the wrong people running that authority. This is an interesting challenge for their HR director.

How to formulate an HR strategy without a business strategy

When all the questions about strategic thinking and planning have been asked you may come to the conclusion that the business is actually in 'default strategy mode', otherwise known as no strategy mode. This is a great opportunity for HR.

First, someone has to have enough credibility and authority to point out to the board that they are not following any clearly defined strategy.

When this is expressed in HR terms it helps to add weight. For example, does the company want a 'pile 'em high, sell 'em cheap' approach or will it pursue a 'customer centred' philosophy? These options require entirely different types of culture. Yet, without a clear strategy, how does the organisation know what type of people it needs to recruit? What training and development should it be offering? Do we want call centre operators or do we need people who have to think for themselves and use their judgement?

The big problem with 'default strategies' is that they are easily knocked off course when external factors force the company to change its ways. The public sector is a very good example of this general point. The normal default strategy for the head of a civil service department or local government organisation is to do whatever is demanded of them and generally to keep their political masters happy. Then, when the latest government decided to introduce the concept of 'best value', they were very poorly prepared to face up to this challenge. There are obviously very few leaders in the public sector who have had strategies to deliver what taxpayers, like me and you, should always have been entitled to expect anyway. Now they have to be forced to give us real value for money. However, from the HR perspective, when they have to change course it is not so easy to change the people. Organisations are like supertankers: they take a great deal of time to change direction. Have public sector employees been selected and developed to want to deliver best value?

The same issues arise in the commercial sector. One very large and well known financial services company in the UK had a reputation for employing 'foot in the door' sales tactics. When the mountain of financial services legislation outlawed such practices they realised they had to change. However, this required a fundamental shift in thinking. Their initial attempts to address the new regulations were not far

---

reaching enough. They needed to engineer a complete break with the past. They were never going to do this without both a clear business strategy and a closely linked HR strategy. Two HR directors came and went in swift succession because they did not produce an HR strategy that got to grips with the real issues.

Note

1. David Hussey (1996) *Business Driven HRM*. Chichester: Wiley.

CHAPTER 8

Knowing the difference between fads and fundamentals

Effective HR strategies are about getting the fundamentals right and avoiding following the latest fad or fashion. *The bottom line HR function knows the difference between a fad and a fundamental.*

Why fads persist

However, I mentioned in Chapter 7 how HR directors find it much easier to resort to fads rather than bothering to address the real, fundamental issues. This is why HR teams are so obsessed with the latest gimmicks. This is fully acknowledged by one of the researchers on the latest IPD research project, launched in 1999, to try and establish a connection between strategic HRM and bottom line, organisational performance:

> The more strategic approach to people management has delivered bottom-line results, but we don't know how that

happens. UK management is atrocious in terms of learning and implementation. They virtually never evaluate: it's all done on a whim, thinking, 'What's the latest fad? I must get into that'. (Marc Thompson, Templeton College Oxford)[1]

Do you find this quote as odd as I do? Strategy is about planning to achieve objectives. So how can HR strategists plan to deliver bottom line results through people management if they 'don't know how that happens'? That is a bit like planning to fly from Glasgow to London without knowing if there is an airline that actually covers this route. Or, worse still, waking up in London and wondering how you got there.

Perhaps this research will finally start to make some connections though. Well, it might if the sponsors of the research at the IPD had any apparent faith in it. Look at this quote from the leaders of the project, Ron Collard and Angela Baron, writing about 'HR and the bottom line' in the IPD's own journal, *People Management*, on 14 October 1999:

> We do not expect to be able to give practitioners all the answers. Indeed, it would be a mistake to claim that there is a universal best way of achieving better performance through people management.

With this lack of confidence it is no wonder many HR practitioners fall back on the latest fad or fashion, in the desperate hope that it will help in some way.

Perhaps if we understood this tendency to resort to fads better we might be able to do something about it. So let us pause now and take a very critical look at the modern management disease of busy and hard-pressed CEOs being seduced by quick-fix, simplistic, pre-prepared, ready-made solutions to their most intractable HR problems. I think there are numerous reasons why this problem persists.

'Nobody ever got fired for buying IBM'

You have probably already heard this one. If you are a 'politician', and your sole aim in life is to ensure no mud sticks to you on your climb up the greasy pole, then a standard defensive tactic is to only buy your management ideas from an organisation that has a 'name'. Then, if it goes wrong, at least you can say you did your best by selecting a reputable supplier. Such people have very little interest in what actually works and what does not.

I would have such people on my strategic HR hit-list.

Using off-the-shelf solutions means you don't have to engage the business

The wiser business leaders, and more perceptive HR directors, know that their organisation is full of command and control, blame-type managers. They also know this is not good for business because no one accepts the principle of personal accountability for fear of retribution.

However, knowing what the problem is and finding a solution are two entirely different things. Solving this problem means probably confronting some senior people, firing a few as an example to the others, and addressing the difficult issue of opening up honest dialogue within and between different teams and departments. All of this means 'engaging' the business.

It is much easier, however, to run away from what looks like a difficult, intractable problem by buying in a 360° feedback consultant and their software. Everyone then plays the 360° game of supposedly giving honest and constructive feedback about their peers and colleagues but no one ever really links this with the underlying business problems. So it becomes a pure activity.

It is this *lack of engagement* that probably best characterises a 'fad'. If the business problems are openly acknowledged and owned by those who need to do something about them, then the exercise will not turn out to be a fad.

If you don't support the latest idea you are seen as negative

There is always pressure to follow what the CEO has just said is his next big initiative. In the worst cases this leads to what I call the 'camp guard syndrome' where nobody asks any questions or challenges anything and just blindly follows suit. It is a pity that worries about personal job security can lead to such wasted opportunities and effort.

Analysis is pointless if the solution is off-the-shelf

I have sat through many conference presentations that purport to be case studies of HR 'best practice'. When the fad of 'management competencies' hit the scene some years ago it appeared that, regardless of the business issues, the final HR solution was always the installation of a competence framework.

You do not have to be too sceptical to ask the simple question of whether competencies can be the answer to so many disparate problems. However, a more damning criticism is that if competencies are such a panacea why do we need to hear a long-winded analysis that seems to always lead to such a standard solution?

Irrational approaches are rarely exposed

In India there is a group which calls itself the 'rationalists'. Their aim in life is to expose the false practices of witch-doctors and faith healers in the rural areas of India who exploit the superstitions of the local population, usually for monetary reward. So, for example, the witch doctor may try to drive out evil spirits in a village by making brightly coloured flames and smoke emanate from a fire. He does so by surreptitiously throwing pyrotechnic powder into the fire. The rationalists aim is to expose the false nature of this illusion by creating exactly the same effect themselves and then revealing how the trick works.

I feel a bit like a 'rationalist' in the world of HRM. There are some really weird and wonderful practices out there and I see a great need to expose some of these as the work of charlatans and what the Americans call snake oil merchants. But let us never underestimate the power of superstition and other belief systems. Quite intelligent and rational people will still try to justify the use of a particular technique, either because they do genuinely believe in it or, more likely, because they have already put a great deal of time, effort and money into it and do not want to be made to look stupid.

'Initiative-itis'

Having studied this subject for some time, and having worked with a very wide range of HR people, I do not think it is exaggerating to say that HR has become addicted to launching new initiatives. This has led to initiative 'junkies' who are driven on by the 'high' they get from launching the initiative only to move onto yet another initiative when the buzz wears off. Despite my being one of the greatest critics of HR's obsession with fads I have to admit that my open attacks on them does not seem to have resulted in any significant reduction in the number of new fads that come along each year – particularly, I have to say, from the American market.

I suppose 'initiative-itis' is just continuing proof that hope always triumphs over experience.

Everyone's a guru these days

If we were to look at national characteristics and competencies and you were to ask most Europeans what the Americans were very good at, my guess is that top of the list would be salesmanship. They would sell sand to the Arabs or freezers to the Inuits, as the saying goes. I will never forget my first, face-to-face experience of this national obsession on my very first holiday in America with my family. After a long flight, and feeling slightly disorientated because of the time difference, I went to pick up our hire car only to be regaled with all sorts of options, none of which seemed to be of the least interest to me.

Perhaps the worst 'offer' was the use of a mobile phone during my stay (this was before mobile phones were so widely used). Why I should want to contact anyone or them me on my holiday seemed to be completely contrary to the whole reason for going on holiday in the first place. The Americans know this as well as I do but their national psyche forces them to seize every possible opportunity for a sale.

Although it galls me to say this, I have to admit that another core competence of America is its ability to innovate, probably at a faster rate than any other country in the world. Put these two competencies together and you get a very powerful combination that keeps the cash tills ringing. The only problem is that not all of the 'new' management ideas that have emanated from America over the last 20 years or so have been that brilliant. Perhaps only a small percentage have really been fresh, innovative, ground-breaking and effective. But that does not stop the Americans selling all of their ideas as though they were the greatest thing since sliced bread.

A by-product of all this energy is a huge growth in the number of supposed 'gurus' in America. I do not know if anyone is keeping count but my guess is that it is increasing at an alarming rate. In the HR field this has meant a plethora of approaches that have been sold well but will never deliver.

So, the problem for the unwary business leader, never mind the HR professional, is being able to sort the wheat from the chaff – which of these things work and which do not? How do they choose? Glossy marketing literature and slick sales presentations still seem to convince the less discerning but a better understanding may help.

A secondary, but also important, point is that some new technologies and methodologies have been proved to be effective. So other organisations copy what they think is the same approach only to discover that they did not take the full idea on board or really understand what they were letting themselves in for.

It is difficult to get it right. First you have to choose a workable methodology and then you have to make it work. Unfortunately, in this process there is a great deal of confusion caused and good approaches can get lost among the multitude of approaches on offer. So let us revisit some of the better known management ideas and see which ones are worth trying or at least deserve a second look.

What's the big idea and what's the connection?

In Figure 8.1 there are a whole host of management ideas represented as totally disjointed 'thought bubbles'. However, the basic question is, are they all unconnected ideas or is there a common thread or theme which binds them together into one, overarching, integrated and holistic philosophy?

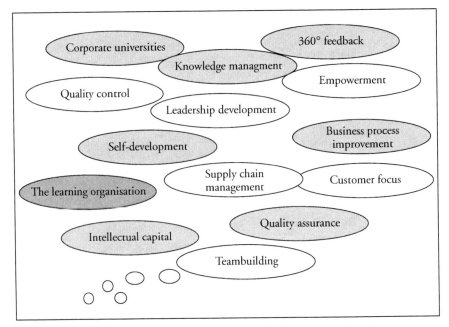

Figure 8.1 What's the big idea and what's the connection?

Is this just a list of fads and fashions from the last 15 years or are they all part of the same, single, total quality management philosophy? My own view is that not only is this not just a list of disparate ideas but most, if not all of them, can be connected as a natural, logical, historical sequence of developments. This sequence may not be absolutely rigid and the exact chronology may differ, but it is relatively easy to see how it has happened in a practical context.

Perhaps we could start by attempting to put a date on them. If we did I think 'quality control' would probably be the first on the list. (By the way, for those readers who are not old enough to know about the history of TQM this might be a helpful summary of how organisations have developed over the last 20 years or so.)

- Quality control

- Quality assurance

- Customer focus

- Teambuilding

- Empowerment

- Self-development

- The learning organisation

- Organisation design

- Supply chain management

- Business process improvement

- 360° feedback

- Knowledge management

- Intellectual capital

- Corporate universities

- Leadership development

To try to put all of these ideas in context I will take my own experience in automotive components manufacturing. About 15 years ago we had to accept that if we wanted to stay in business we had to constantly improve our products and the level of service we offered. We knew little or nothing about total quality management and did not have a strategy or philosophy of continuous improvement. Nevertheless, we had to start somewhere. Under pressure from our biggest customers (including Ford and Vauxhall) we started with basic quality control. We started putting *quality control* inspectors at the end of each production line to make sure the products we made met the quality standards set by our customers.

Only when we did this could we really start to get a true picture of how bad we were. In effect, this was our first serious attempt at quality measurement. Only when we started to understand the size and nature of the problems we faced could we start to do something about them.

However, it was not too long before it become apparent that having quality inspectors at the end of the line was an extra expense we could do without. Plus, they were doing nothing to stop the problems as they occurred in the earliest stages of the production process.

So we naturally moved on from thinking in terms of quality control to the notion of *quality assurance*. We started trying to build quality in at every stage of the process. No one had to tell us this home truth; we learned it for ourselves. However, it would have saved us a great deal of time and effort if someone had taught us this important lesson sooner.

Meanwhile, with a renewed focus on achieving quality standards, pressure mounted and a natural question from some managers was 'so what quality standards do our customers want and how much are they willing to pay?' This is the 'fit-for-purpose' argument that caused us to be more *customer focused*. We began to speak to our customers more regularly, in order to clearly define what quality standard they needed and ensure that the products we made were not over-specified. In other words our focus, inevitably and quite naturally, swung round to the relationship we had with our customers. In the process, our understanding of the term quality changed. Initially we would have defined quality as like a Rolls-Royce. Now we had a much more pragmatic view of what quality was.

While the *external supplier/customer relationships* changed so did *internal relationships*. The drive for quality started to expose weak areas of the organisation and highlighted how internal 'customer' relationships were becoming crucial in quality assurance. For example, the impact of the performance of the 'goods inwards' department could be seen on production schedules if they delayed their checking procedures.

The one good thing that came out of all of this was that we did start to see some immediate improvements, primarily because we were more aware of the problems we had. After a time, though, most of the immediate, simple, obvious production problems were resolved and we began to find it more difficult to find ways to improve quality or reduce costs further. To progress along the continuous improvement road we hit up against some fundamental HR issues. First, supervisors, quality assurance staff and managers were not skilled enough at analysing the causes of the more intractable quality problems and therefore had no means for solving them. Second, the command and control style hierarchy that we still had produced a culture where everyone still tended to look after their own turf and were happy enough to pass the buck whenever possible.

This culture had managed to keep the company in business for many years but its deficiencies were now being starkly exposed. It was getting in the way of effectively resolving problems that could only be resolved through coordinated and cooperative cross-functional action. This pressure shifted our focus again, this time to a greater need for *teambuilding and teamworking*. We also had to provide them with problem-solving tools and techniques and I actually remember being part of the first brainstorming session. But there were many more techniques that we regarded as the toolkit of total quality management (TQM) programmes (Pareto, cause and effect, failure analysis, etc.) and we had to train our people how to use these techniques.

If we can now digress slightly for a moment, it is interesting how many organisations have seen poor teamworking as the main cause of all their business woes. Consequently, they spend inordinate amounts of time, energy and expenditure in this area without seeing it as a particular stage in this overall sequence. Also, many teambuilding programmes, often run as outdoor management programmes, focus on matters such as team spirit and bonding, without ever trying to make this happen in the workplace. No wonder so many of these programmes fail to make any difference.

As the months and years rolled by the evolutionary learning process continued to grind on and at some stage it began to dawn on some members of the management team that they could not possibly 'manage in' quality all the time, especially when they were entirely at the mercy of the skills, capabilities and attitudes of operators on the production line. So to achieve even further improvement the operators themselves had to be brought into the loop more and become more involved in the quality assurance process. They too would have to be trained to identify problems and *empowered* to put them right as soon as possible. This caused a great deal of angst among middle managers whose felt that their very existence was threatened. It was not an easy road but the wheels were most definitely in perpetual motion by now.

The more we devolved accountability and responsibility to those on the line the more we realised that many of them were incapable of using the problem-solving tools and techniques. After all, they had been recruited as lowly production operators and many had not attained a very high academic standard of education. They were unable, for example, to produce simple histograms. Hence questions were now being asked about how well state education was preparing future generations of workers for the new world order.

So great effort went into training and developing operators, except that some of them, being on the bottom rung of the organisational ladder and having never been asked for an input before, were totally disenchanted with the company and saw no reason why they should adopt a different attitude. This led us at the time, I have to admit unconsciously, to review the fundamental relationship that had developed between employer and employee. Little did we know it but we had stumbled across the concept of the *psychological contract.*

We were in a heavily unionised environment and the bad old days of British industrial relations were not yet a thing of the dim and distant past. I would not describe the relations with the union as totally confrontational by any means but they were certainly not totally cooperative either. If we were to continue to make great strides forward we would have to reassess the 'deal' that we had established with our employees. We could not expect ever-increasing commitment from them without offering a more enlightened way of managing.

We needed to make our workforce more flexible and more able to resolve problems as they arose. This required a level of development in each individual that was difficult to identify for everyone. Hence, it was a natural move towards promoting the notion of *self-development* rather than just training courses. Companies like Ford took this idea to the stage where they offered all employee £500 to put towards their own development needs. In many other industries there was a growth in company learning centres, where employees could find out all they needed to know on a wide range of topics. There would be videos, management books, self-instructional texts and all types of learning materials. Those who eagerly took to this opportunity soon found themselves in a situation where the lines between working, training and learning had become very blurred. This, for me, was when we saw the first stirrings of what we now call a *learning organisation* (at the far right, high added value but aspirational end of the HRM scale in Figure 2.1).

This brief run-through obviously skirts around many of the issues that arise during the journey of continuous improvement. Like many long-term processes it is much easier to notice patterns and understand developments after the event than it is at the time. Speak to anyone in an organisation going through these changes and no doubt they will refer to the need to change their command and control, blame culture because operational pressures demand such fundamental changes.

Organisations that instigate explicit, off-the-shelf 'culture change' programmes to bring about such changes are missing the point. The change has to happen sequentially and in an evolutionary way. The only other alternative is revolution. Admittedly this can be just as effective in achieving strategic organisational goals (some will remember Times Newspapers moving to Wapping and in one fell swoop ridding themselves of years of bad industrial relations problems) but it is usually more violent and bloody in the short term.

The pressures that all of this places on organisation structures are often imperceptible but no less real for that. They eventually start to highlight the need for new *organisation designs*. The benefits of rigid hierarchical organisation structures are bound to come under scrutiny when operators require less and less supervision and are empowered to make their own decisions. *Supply chain management* demands that the chain be as straightforward and efficient as possible, especially when there is a customer requirement for just-in-time delivery. Anyone who has ever had to move to this way of working will have seen the stresses that it can place on production and despatch personnel.

Eventually, all of this leads to a total reassessment of the actual *core business processes* themselves to see if they can be streamlined or made more effective, hence the drive towards *business process re-engineering* – which again automatically means organisation redesign.

Fundamentals add value, fads don't

The one thing that all of the idea bubbles in Figure 8.1 have in common is that they stemmed from an attempt to maximise organisational and customer value through a very systematic and focused approach to generating never ending improvements. It just so happens that in this process there are what some HR people would regard as beneficial by-products such as greater employee involvement, personal development and growth. But these are just that, by-products – they were never intended to be the ultimate purpose of TQM.

What is more, all of these initiatives should be installed to achieve *measurable, bottom line improvements*. Over a considerable period of time there should be a perceptible and tangible change in the organisation. The operating efficiency of the organisation should improve dramatically, cycle times and product development times should improve and the organisation structure will, itself, be decidedly different. Customer satisfaction should increase and customer complaints and errors should fall. All of these are clearly observable when the requisite measures are put in place.

A more subtle, but equally crucial, point is that if these developments are badly synchronised or in the wrong sequence, then the realisation of any potential benefits will be severely restricted. Maybe this is why many of the 'latest-thinking, management guru' concepts never achieve anything like the promises made by their most enthusiastic proponents. This is why they then become regarded as just another in a long line of latest management fads.

For example, how many organisations have attempted a fundamental BPR programme without having supported its employees through a process of self-development and empowerment? Yet without these pre-conditions the real benefits of BPR, which come from giving people new roles in more effective processes, are unlikely to be realised. It is interesting that much of the criticism currently directed at BPR initiatives centres around their failure to fully understand the people implications of redesigning core processes.

TQM is just common sense applied systematically. It is based on some fundamental, unassailable principles such as needing to analyse cause and effect and having measures in place to provide feedback and generate improvement. Adhering to these principles religiously and relentlessly gives birth to the learning organisation.

The longer-term implications of continuous improvement

The real *raison d'être* for the learning organisation is, first and foremost, a business proposition. At its simplest level the basic questions are, how do we keep ahead of the competition in terms of cost base, productivity and quality and be totally responsive to the market in terms of product development cycles and time-to-market lead times?

These became the new commercial realities and as the dust from the first bout of rapid change began to clear it was becoming apparent that a 'new' type of organisation was required, even if no one could articulate exactly what that new organisation would look like.

In the short to medium term, command and control organisations can, of course, continue to thrive (there are still many examples around), especially while margins allow them to. But as the longer term approaches, those organisations which manage to unleash the full talents of their people and prove to be exceptionally responsive to market changes will have managed to gain a significant competitive advantage.

The learning organisation may not be the *only* way to achieve such advantages but those organisations which do not adopt this philosophy will be struggling to come up with a viable alternative. We are entering an era where people really are being seen as the only true source of competitive advantage left. How that resource is managed and developed, therefore, is crucial. Perhaps, at some stage in the not-too-distant future, the learning organisation will indeed become a fundamental of commercial existence rather than just another management philosophy.

In the meantime, we have seen the birth of *360° feedback* systems, *knowledge management* and an awareness of the importance of *intellectual capital*. Why? Well the real reason is because they sound sexy and are being sold as universal panaceas. This is a pity because the concepts themselves are very sound. Many organisations need to move away from being blame cultures because it makes them less efficient and effective than they could be. It stifles innovation and creativity. People are afraid to make mistakes so they err on the side of caution, failing to make decisions when they should. Such organisations need to open themselves up to new ideas and constructive criticism from within. 360° feedback is one attempt to facilitate such a transformation. The idea is right but the execution rarely accomplishes what it sets out to achieve.

An HR director I knew in a large airline service company wanted to try out 360° feedback on some of his senior management colleagues. So he set up a pilot (no pun intended) exercise with some management volunteers. Actually the 'volunteers' were skilfully selected to represent the 'best and worst' managers. As a result of this experiment he found that the 'good' managers got excellent feedback from all their peers and colleagues while the 'bad' managers received, as was expected, pretty stinging indictments of their management style and behaviour.

Needless to say, the good managers did not change their behaviour because it was positively reinforced while the bad managers chose to completely disregard the evidence that was staring them in the face. Consequently the whole exercise was a complete waste of time, even if the good managers did achieve a very pleasant boost to their esteem.

The obvious connection between knowledge management (KM) and our evolutionary sequence is that a well-developed organisation, which has already squeezed every last drop of value out of its business, is always looking at new ways of achieving continuous improvement. One obvious target is to make sure everyone shares their knowledge and experience with each other as much as possible, so that no opportunities for improvement are missed. This should happen naturally but to help it along, many companies are now putting a great deal of effort into capturing all the knowledge floating around inside the organisation.

Intellectual capital (IC) is a variation on a similar theme. Here, all the good ideas and inherent creativity and innovation in the workforce is supposedly tapped. Some have gone on to try and measure how much intellectual capital is contributing to the balance sheet. This seems a rather facile endeavour to me. Genuinely creative and innovative organisations allow people to contribute as much as they can and the results show up in improved performance figures (which was always the objective anyway), so trying to measure intellectual capital seems to miss the point somewhat.

The irony in all of these last three concepts, 360°, KM and IC, is that a conscious, explicit attempt to use these concepts is probably one of the greatest indicators that they are unlikely to succeed. As with our evolutionary story, in the best organisations these things happen subconsciously. Visionary leaders like Eiji Toyoda understand the interrelationships between all of these ideas and work at putting a culture in place to allow them to blossom. I'm not a gardener but it's a bit like the difference between dumping three tons of manure on the garden in the hope that it will help things to flourish when a bit of patient and caring husbandry in the long run will have a much more beneficial and enduring effect.

Evidence of the learning organisation

Would you know a learning organisation if you saw one? How about this as an indicator: I asked my contact at Toyota what would be the shortest time needed to change a production process, from initial identification of the opportunity right through to physically changing the process. Before I give you the answer I wonder how long it would take to change a business process in your organisation? I often get answers to this question of anywhere between one and six months. Some people say it is virtually impossible trying to change processes because it gets too involved.

The answer I got from Toyota was three hours! If this happens regularly (and there is ample evidence that it does) just think of the competitive advantage such changes are building up against their competitors over many years. More importantly, consider what type of organisation allows such rapid change to happen and imagine how long it probably took to get there. The production operator who identified the initial improvement opportunity had to *want* to spot such an opportunity. He also had to have the capability of doing so. The supervisor had to have a relationship with the operator, which ensured they did not obstruct the new idea and were happy to pursue it to its conclusion. Moreover, higher management levels had to be available and willing to respond to the idea quickly and then be allowed to make whatever decisions were necessary.

There is a complex combination of factors here that allows the organisation to learn and, simultaneously, benefit from this learning in hard terms (cost reduction, improved process cycle times, etc.). The personnel systems, organisation structure, values, culture and many other factors all have a part to play in allowing this organisation to learn and adapt at very quick speeds. All of this can only come together if the HR strategy has created a totally integrated, holistic people management system.

Applying this scenario to your own organisation can begin to give an indication of how far down the learning organisation road you may be. Ask yourself, are employees, at all levels, sufficiently encouraged or motivated to even want to suggest improvement ideas? Furthermore, how good would those ideas be? For every good one would there be many bad ones? And yet, if you are new to this, you cannot foster idea generation without freeing up all ideas. This, in turn, cannot be achieved without creating an atmosphere that eliminates the fear of ridicule or censure for those whose ideas fall at the first hurdle.

If you get past this barrier to what extent do employees have the wherewithal to analyse the situation and sift good ideas from bad? What tools or techniques have they been trained in for doing so? If the idea is a genuinely beneficial one how long would it take for a higher level of management to give the green light? Moreover, would they also have a systematic way of ensuring one process change did not have a deleterious effect on other processes elsewhere in the organisation?

Any delays or obstacles at any stage in this improvement process are each an indicator of issues that would have to be addressed if you were to move towards becoming a learning organisation.

Interestingly, negative attitudes by senior managers to implementing new ideas would be one of the most difficult to address. This could only be done by instilling the sort of values and culture that the learning organisation demands. Getting the culture and values right is not an intangible goal though. It is very tangibly going to bring about hard, bottom line improvements – the sort of improvements that will keep the organisation ahead in its chosen markets, or, at the very least, that will allow it to continue playing in its chosen game.

Note

1.   Quoted in the *Sunday Times*, 31 October 1999.

PART 3

HR as the performance management function

CHAPTER 9

The performance-focused HR function

Perhaps we should not read too much into magazine articles but I was fascinated by the title of this one:

> 'Measuring the intangible. Performance criteria in jobs without a bottom line.'[1]

I may have been critical of the present leadership of the IPD but when we look at this article we can see how much worse it was in the past. The whole idea that there is such a thing as a 'job without a bottom line' is ludicrous. No doubt many organisations have people doing work of little or no value but Barry Curnow was arguing that you cannot measure performance in some jobs by using normal business metrics. Is it any wonder that many personnel practitioners do not see their role as having anything to do with bottom line improvement?

In my experience, the bottom line HR function does not currently exist. I have argued why I believe this to be the case. However, by this stage in the book, plenty of evidence has been presented to demonstrate that organisations are seriously in need of such an HR function. My belief, therefore, is that it will exist sooner or later. But what exactly is it?

A definition of the bottom line HR function

The bottom line HR function's role is to analyse, identify and make explicit the connections between the organisation's strategic and operational objectives and its human resource. Where necessary it needs to transform the human resource capability to meet those challenges. It will do so by defining performance standards and offering methods for improving performance to maximise each individual's contribution to organisational goals by helping them to fully realise their added-value potential.

If an HR function is going to fulfil this role then the people who work in the function have to have some way of working out what, exactly, are the connections between the performance of employees, both as individuals and team members, and organisational goals. If you have followed the arguments presented here so far then, hopefully, you will agree that simplistic assumptions such as 'look after your people and they will look after the business' are inaccurate and do not offer a solid basis for developing HR policies.

The two most important elements needed for a bottom line HR function to operate are:

- employee performance measurement, with meaningful measures; and

- actually managing the human resource as a resource, not in the woolly-minded way that most personnel professionals approach the task.

At its simplest level, this means looking at people as a genuine resource which has to show an acceptable return. The most positive message here, especially to the finance director, is that cutting people costs cannot be undertaken without simultaneously considering the 'debit' side of the transaction. That is, if we get rid of part of the human resource we might save cost but, ultimately, what happens to overall organisational value? Equally, though, any increase in expenditure on human resources should be able to indicate an acceptable return on investment (ROI).

This is not just a case of promoting the business perspective of the HR function. It is just as much to do with ensuring everyone sees HR as a business function. The use of business language and terminology is crucial to the success of the bottom line HR function.

The language of performance

One language that every organisation now speaks is the language of performance, individual and organisational. If people really are a source of sustainable, competitive advantage then their performance has to be optimised. This, in turn, requires effective performance measures and methods for improving performance. If the HR function is to offer this service then its effectiveness will be measured (and evaluated) in relation to how much it improves performance. Never before has HR had such an opportunity to put itself on the map.

As we have already seen, though, HR is well known for its resistance to and lack of capability in measurement. Yet everything the HR function does should have an impact on measurable performance improvement. HR should aim to recruit good performers, train employees to perform better, reward and recognise superior performance and deal with underperformance. So a function, whose *raison d'être* is maximising employee performance, should not only be good at performance measures, they should be the experts.

This is a fantastic opportunity for HR because every other function has failed to deliver the goods in performance measurement. The accountants have finally acknowledged that their measurement systems are historic and do not address the broader issues of human capital and the knowledge worker. The operations and sales directors can no longer infer that the only measures that count are theirs.

The bottom line HR function, therefore, will be the employee performance measurement and management function.

Performance measurement and management

Performance measurement and management, both in theory and practice, are areas that still tax the best minds of most organisations. Many attempts have been made to produce a robust methodology that can deliver maximum employee potential. There are no simple answers but any budding HR consultant would do well to make sure they are fully abreast of the literature and the case studies on this subject. The HR consultant who can master this subject will always be in great demand and should attract the rewards and status that will inevitably be offered to those who can help maximise organisational performance.

Some years ago I was invited by one of my clients, who worked in a large NHS trust hospital in the UK, to meet her boss, the HR director, to talk about the use of measurement in HR. It was not long before I was conscious that my questions to him were making him feel very uncomfortable and he moved onto the defensive very quickly. The discussion was about his new performance management system, which had been installed for about 12 months. It was pretty obvious that it was not going very well, or even as planned. He was willing to accept this but remarked: 'It's not my fault that it isn't working. All I can do is design the system and then leave managers to use it correctly. If they don't use it properly then it's not my problem.' This sort of arrogance had led to his total abdication from responsibility or accountability.

I replied that I was not interested in who was at fault. However, if avoiding blame was the main objective of any initiative then that, in itself, told me a great deal about the organisational culture at this hospital. This did not make him feel any better and he remained firmly on the defensive. In my most reassuring tone (which took a great deal of effort on my part) I said that if we could get away from the blame culture maybe we could do something about getting the performance management system back on track. This generated no interest whatsoever.

My final shot was that, regardless of who was at fault, the performance management system, in its present form, was adding no value. All of his effort would therefore be wasted. This was the final nail in the discussion and the meeting ended shortly afterwards. And we wonder why there are still long waiting lists in the NHS.

It is amazing how easily our focus can be sidetracked by blame. Yet surely the main point of this story is that, whatever else this HR director was doing, he was certainly adding no value through the performance initiative. His time on this was completely wasted. Actually it is worse than that – time and effort that does not add value must, by definition, be sapping value from the hospital. The saddest part of all of this is that the one area in which HR should add lots of value – performance management – is an area in which it traditionally has had little to offer.

Performance management consulting

In Figure 9.1 the basic proposition on performance measurement and management is encapsulated. First, individual employee performance has to be measured. Only when it has been measured can it be managed.

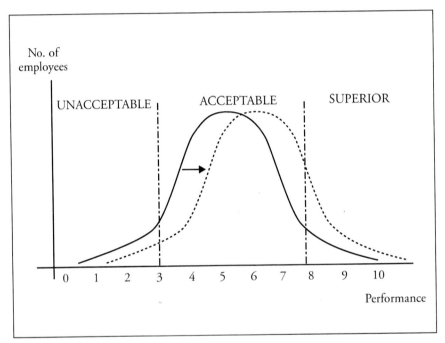

Figure 9.1 The performance measurement and management proposition.

Regardless of the actual performance measures used, assuming you do so on a reasonable scale (I always recommend something like a 1 to 10 scale), the measures are likely to produce a curve like the one shown in Figure 9.1. This is a normal, bell-shaped, distribution curve. It could be skewed one way or the other but that does not matter because the only reason for producing this curve is to shift it to the right (the dotted curve).

If you want try this out in practice it is very easy to ask a group of managers to just give their staff an 'all-in' score of between 1 and 10, having already told them that 3 or less is unacceptable and 8 or over means superior performance. If you do this you may well find that the curve is skewed to the right, starting from the 3 mark. (What manager is going to admit they have underperformers in their team, especially if they have been in the team for some time?)

There is often a tendency to over-score because many managers do not want to have to face up to managing underperformance. In such cases it is worth pointing out to the managers concerned that it is better to start with lower scores because this will mean it is easier to show an improvement. The object of the exercise, do not forget, is to shift the curve, not the blame.

From the HR practitioner's point of view, until these measures are in place they do not have a very clear basis for consulting on performance issues. If, for example, a manager said all of his team scored 7 or above then shifting that part of the curve may involve reward, recognition and career development issues. On the other hand, those scoring around the 2 to 4 mark may well require remedial help and support. The performance curve not only enables the HR team to focus on performance issues but it provides a basis of measurement for demonstrating improvement and improved added value.

Some would argue that there is nothing new in the idea of performance management. While this is essentially true, what is different now is that organisations that are already performing very well need to continue to improve their performance even further. In terms of Figure 9.1, the employee who scores an acceptable 4 this year will find that this is the minimum standard necessary next year when the goalposts have moved.

Critical elements of a performance management function

Having just provided a brief introduction to employee performance measurement and management the subject is obviously a lot more complex than just producing some simple metrics.

Employee performance is the number one priority for the bottom line HR function. Here, we have just looked at a few key elements of performance and how it affects the role of the HR function. For a much more detailed guide and the sort of in-depth treatment that this subject deserves see the author's *Measuring and Managing Employee Performance.*[2]

Notes

1.   Title of an article written by Barry Curnow, the then President of the Institute of Personnel Management (now the IPD), from *Human Resources* magazine, Summer 1991.

2.   Paul Kearns (2000) *Measuring and Managing Employee Performance – A practical manual to maximise organisational performance through people.* London: Financial Times/Prentice Hall.

CHAPTER 10

The added value HR function

In the previous chapter we considered the role that HR can play in performance measurement and management. This is just one, albeit extremely important, aspect of the bottom line HR function.

Whatever role HR is to play it should, above all else, aim to be a high added value function. In order to achieve this aim HR practitioners have to have a very clear understanding of what added value is and how they can create greater value through HRM. They also have to chose to go down the added value road.

The proverbial fork in the HR road

Essentially, HR can choose to offer maximum value or it can retreat into its administrative shell. In Chapter 1 we heard from Thomas Stewart why he thought personnel had an awful reputation. In the same article he summed up the stark choice now facing HR.

HR has come to the proverbial fork in the road. One leads to a highly automated employee-services operation ... The other leads straight to the CEO's office.[1]

If we only look at how critical Stewart is we might miss his main point that the second option presents HR with a fantastic opportunity.

Actually, Stewart was commenting on the growing trend in the USA to outsource non-core activities but with particular reference to the HR function. How prescient were Stewart's observations back in 1996? Well, look at these comments from *Personnel Today* on 10 June 1999, under the headline 'Generalist posts go in reshuffle'. It was reported that:

Industrial giant the BOC Group is scrapping all HR generalist jobs in an overhaul aimed at saving up to £10 m worldwide ... a new HR service centre will carry out administrative duties.

Perhaps BOC did not think about the subject as deeply as Thomas Stewart. It could be that a simple look at HR costs was enough to convince the board to embark on a reshuffle to increase economies of scale. As a result, they decided to set up an HR services centre to provide basic personnel administration as efficiently as possible. The big question raised here, though, is does BOC really understand the potential added value of HR? Or does it really just expect it to offer a low-value, support service?

Focusing on value generation and the bottom line

I have met enough personnel people, both as work colleagues and on my travels, to know that the vast majority of them never came into the profession to get seriously involved at the sharp end of the business.

They probably chose personnel precisely for the opposite reason. Worse still, their main justification was that they 'like working with people'. This is why many of them have been having an identity crisis. They are struggling to reconcile their interest in looking after the organisation's people with driving improved performance and trying to squeeze every last ounce of value from the business. The two objectives seem incompatible and, as we saw in Chapter 1, the Director-General of the IPD, in my opinion, does not seem to be giving them a clear steer in this regard.

Yet here am I recommending, very strongly, that they focus all their attention on value generation and the bottom line. 'Value' here refers to bottom line value – that is, profits. It is also, however, referring to improved shareholder value through improved organisational performance. All functions (finance, marketing, R&D, PR, etc.) are now trying to answer the questions, 'how do we add value and how can we add more value?' However, despite all the talk about it, very rarely does anyone sit down and actually define what added value is. So let us define what we mean by added value.

In Figure 10.1 we are looking at a brewery in its current year (the box on the left) and in the coming year (the box on the right). First, the brewery company has to decide what it regards as the 'value' of the business. This could be expressed in many ways other than simple profit. Here we see a combination of market share, share price, volume of beer sold and revenue generated. All of these are measurable and all could be expressed in £/$s (e.g. £/$1 bn of a £/$5 bn market, share price (£/$) or market capitalisation in £/$ m, and volume and revenue would be virtually the same as the £/$1 bn market share). The simple question then is how do these value indicators improve from year 1 to year 2? If they move up then we can say that the brewery has increased its value. However, if brewing productivity increases by 10 per cent but the brewery market share falls by 15 per cent then the net result is more likely to be a reduction in value.

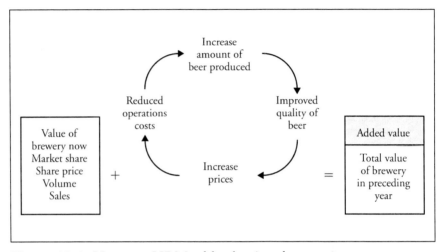

Figure 10.1 How can HRM add value in a brewery?

I used a brewery as our first example of added value to show how the concept can apply in any profit-focused organisation. However, exactly the same concept can be adapted in the public and not-for-profit sectors. It is an extremely adaptable and powerful concept and yet it is of great practical use as well.

Figure 10.2, however, is intended to illustrate what added value is for a hospital. What is the current value of the services the hospital provides now (the box on the left of the diagram)? You may find that difficult to answer so let me see if I can use the concept of value to help.

How many patients does this hospital treat each year? Let us say it is 50,000. Would we automatically say this hospital has increased its value (or added more value) if next year it treated 55,000 patients (a 10 per cent increase)? It is not as simple as that, is it? Well, perhaps we need some more information. First, what was the average cost of treating a patient? If it was £1,000 last year and this year it is £1,200 it would be difficult to argue that the hospital had become more valuable or had added greater value. On the basis of these simple figures its value is declining because it is treating less patients for each £1,000 it spends. But even that is too simplistic.

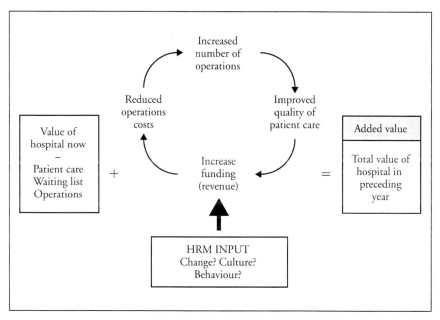

Figure 10.2 How can HRM add value in a hospital?

Perhaps we need to look at this from another angle – the quality of patient care or how many patients were successfully treated. This, in turn, leads to a discussion about what our definition of 'quality of patient care' is. The total quality experts would argue 'fit-for-purpose' – in other words, the expected patient outcomes with the minimum amount of time in hospital. This balances cost and quality.

If this were a private hospital the only other option would be to try and achieve higher prices for its services (increased revenue). You might immediately think that this is nothing to do with the value of the service this hospital provides, but it is. We could argue that the hospital, in the long term, will only be able to charge what people will pay. In other words people pay a price up to the equivalent of their perceived value of the service they get. In the UK, even NHS hospitals will now have to compare themselves with other NHS hospitals on the basis of value.

Value is a tricky concept but the whole point of focusing on it is that it will tell us whether an organisation is improving or not. If the chief executive decided the hospital needed a new coat of paint would this automatically add value? Only if the patients (and relatives?) valued this, and we would only know this if we asked them. So even the more 'intangible' elements of organisational value can only be truly assessed in terms of what customers want and are prepared to pay for. This is why it is such an important concept.

There are numerous options for any organisation to consider when they decide what comprises value. Look at what might constitute value in a hospital: speed of getting a bed, a truly caring culture, pure efficiency, good customer service or just bed usage. These may not be mutually exclusive but sometimes, at an operational level, they are. Efficiency and a caring culture may not sit happily together. This is why it is particularly important, from an HR perspective, to try and get broad agreement among the hospital board as to what they regard as valuable (patient care or volume of patients). It is equally important for clear objectives to be set for all employees based on this definition of value. Otherwise the 'caring culture' nurse may be at loggerheads with the super-efficient staff nurse. Managing this balance is critical if the hospital is to enhance its value to society.

Added value might now appear to be a really difficult concept to put into practice but it has immense importance in its practical application. Rome was not built in a day and no organisation is going to maximise its value overnight but it should be clearly heading in the right direction. So, if in the current year bed usage has to increase by 10 per cent then all employees must accept this as a performance target, but the added value argument says they should not let costs increase by more than 10 per cent. The value concept keeps everyone working towards the same ends and, if they achieve their performance targets, they should be able to go home at night confident and satisfied that they have really done a good job.

But who decides what value the organisation is to focus on? Well, obviously the chairman, CEO and the board of directors will normally decide what value means for the organisation. They will normally decide whether to go for long-term value (e.g. building a brand and reputation) or short-term value (e.g. milking any cash cows but with minimal investment). However, shareholders also have a say in the matter. They will want to see evidence that their shareholding is growing in value. From an HR point of view all that matters is that the focus of value is agreed.

One final point about added value. If we are looking for meaningful, hard data about HR's contribution to added value then only the sort of hard data on the variables shown in Figures 10.1 and 10.2 will do. Hard data is needed to produce hard measures. Only added value data will provide added value measures.

HRM and added value

Figure 10.2 also starts to introduce HRM into the equation because if HRM is not focusing on adding value then what is it doing? Interestingly, HR teams are often tasked with bringing about organisational change through their efforts to modify behaviour and change attitudes. These appear to be completely unmeasurable objectives in added value terms. How much difference, for example, would a change management programme generate? Some HR people would scoff at the very idea of trying to link the two.

Surely, though, that is exactly what HR should be trying to do. First it should articulate everything it does within a framework of added value. It should not embark on any initiative unless the added value goal is clear and already measurable. (For example, if market share is key then is this already measured accurately enough and can it be remeasured easily enough without incurring a high cost?)

There are many good reasons why HR should adopt the added value mantle. It will enable them to:

- speak the language of the business;

- articulate nebulous ideas in tangible terms;

- demonstrate their contribution;

- focus their own initiatives on the things that really matter.

The bottom line function is a high added value function. But it can only add value if it knows what it is. This probably explains why personnel and HR functions, heretofore, have added little if any value – they never really understood what value was and how to create it. If HR people have vague notions about how they might add value they will inevitably become involved in vague and unfocused HR activities. Clarity of objectives is everything. There are two choices: business-focused activity (e.g. we must get our costs down) or HR-focused activity (e.g. we must get this 360° feedback system in).

It is absolutely critical to get on the right track at the beginning. Once you have gone down the HR activity track it is very difficult to get back. You can only get on the business-focused track at the beginning of discussions into organisational problems, issues and opportunities. Also, let us not forget human nature. Who wants to admit they have just embarked on an initiative that has later proved to be unfocused and delivering little or no value?

One final story

A few years ago I was invited to tender for some work with an insurance underwriting syndicate group in the City in London. We all know of the serious problems experienced by the Lloyds insurance market when it came very close to collapse. One long-term consequence of this is that the whole sector has been going through a process of rationalisation with a series of large mergers taking place. This, in turn, resulted in underwriting companies having to adopt some decent, modern management practices. The personnel director at this particular group was asked by the board to set up a more formal system of training and development.

As soon as I met the personnel director I asked for more information on the business, including a copy of the last annual report and the last monthly accounts. He was quite surprised and asked why I needed this information to quote for some training work (he was not a bottom line HR person). Despite his reservations he agreed to send me just a copy of the annual report.

I subsequently made a presentation to a team of his colleagues who were a steering group to introduce better training and development. At this meeting I remarked that, according to the annual report, the underwriting side of the business showed losses on all of its lines of business (e.g. marine, aviation and motor insurance). This simple comment obviously surprised and concerned this group (and we wonder why Lloyds was in such a mess). Fortunately, a lady in the team, albeit slightly put out by my remarks, agreed that the business made its money out of investing the premiums, not out of underwriting per se.

Once I had some acknowledgement of the facts I asked whether we should focus the training and development on the underwriters or the investment team? It seemed obvious to me that there was so much room for improvement in underwriting that the business was bound to benefit from focusing some attention on this area.

I did not get the contract. The personnel director informed me that I was 'too powerful' for them. Perhaps if the Lloyds insurance market had had a bottom line HR function some years ago it would still be a world leader.

Note

1. Thomas A. Stewart (1996) 'Taking on the last bureaucracy', *Fortune* magazine, 15 January.

Appendices

APPENDIX A

Are you a high added value HR practitioner?

A self-assessment primer

HRM can only add real value if those who work in it are operating in a strategically positioned HR function, are happy in a business-focused role and have developed an advanced level skill-set. This questionnaire is intended to prompt you to consider your own role, the skills you have and the *potential* added value that you can generate. If you can answer all of these questions clearly and confidently, without reference to any other documents, then you are working from a position in which you can develop into a high added value practitioner.

But before you start, please note that none of the questions below ask you how much you know about such matters as job evaluation, appraisal systems, management development techniques or any other conventional list of HR activities.

Business analysis

1. Can you list three key components of your organisation's current business strategy?

2. Name three business targets for the current year and one each for years 2 and 3 of the business plan.

3. Can you name three quality improvement targets for your products or services?

4. What is the annual turnover and profit of your business? What was it last year and what is the plan for next year? If you do not work in the commercial sector, what level of funding do you receive and where does it come from?

Business processes

1. What is the definition of a business process?

2. Are you able to produce a process flow diagram?

3. Is your HR function organised along process lines?

4. Name two core processes in your organisation.

Organisation design

1. What do you understand by the term 'organisation design'?

2. What are the main differences between silo, functional and matrix organisations?

3. What comes first when an organisation is being established or restructured, process or structure?

Total quality management

Which of the following analytical techniques are you capable of using in an HR context?

- Pareto analysis
- Cause and effect analysis
- Failure analysis
- Statistical process control

Total quality in HR

1. Do you have a continuous improvement system in place for HR?

2. Do you know what feedback loops are and does your function use them?

3. To what extent is HR activity currently measured?

4. How closely is HR activity focused on and linked to the business plan and the bottom line?

Performance management

1. Do you currently measure individual performance?

2. Do you have a performance management system and is it focused on improving existing performance measures?

3. Do you know the difference between performance and added value?

And finally…

1. Do you regard these questions as relevant to your present position and/or your future development?

2. If you have found these questions difficult to answer, how and when will you start to develop better answers?

APPENDIX B

Identifying the key elements of your business and HR strategies

There are some key strategic questions that are fundamental to effective HR functions such as:

- does your organisation have a clear business strategy?

- does your HR function have a clear strategy?

- are the two strategies closely linked?

- how will you know that the HR strategy is working?

Attempts must be made to answer these questions.

The objectives of the exercise

1.   Write down, as briefly as possible, *three* of your organisation's key strategic objectives.

2.   Write down, as briefly as possible, *three* of your HR function's key strategic objectives.

3.   Indicate any links or connections between 1 and 2 above.

Some guidelines to help you

1. Think in terms of your organisation's products/services, its markets and its financial indices.

2. Think also in terms of Key Performance Indicators (KPIs), Key Result Areas (KRAs) and Critical Success Factors (CSFs).

3. Does HR really have a strategy or is it just a series of policies, procedures and ad hoc initiatives?

4. What measures docs HR use to gauge its effectiveness?

APPENDIX C

Kearns's simple test of HR effectiveness

As we have seen throughout this book, HR teams have an unfortunate habit of launching an initiative and asking questions later. They then have a problem trying to post-rationalise or justify their actions. The sort of initiatives that spring to mind include competence frameworks, 360° feedback, performance related pay, most leadership and management development programmes and even HR measurement systems themselves.

We could spend a great deal of time and effort trying to measure what difference such activities have made. There is a much simpler and quicker way to deal with such unfocused initiatives, though. This simple test comprises three questions which should be answered in the order in which they are shown below. Only if you can confidently put ticks in column A for all three questions can there be any chance of this initiative having contributed anything worthwhile. Any ticks in column B suggest you could have spent your time and effort more fruitfully elsewhere.

Name of initiative: installing a 360° feedback system

	Question	A	B
1.	What has the initiative achieved for the organisation so far? (i.e. cost reduction? output increase? price improvement? measurable quality improvement?)	We believe it has made a difference although we cannot clearly measure it.	As far as we know it has achieved nothing of any significance.
2.	What was this initiative trying to achieve in terms of clearly stated business objectives? (i.e. cost reduction? output increase? price improvement? measurable quality improvement?)	We had stated the objectives of this initiative very clearly at the outset.	We did not state any clear business objectives at the outset.
3.	Was the design of the initiative based on any solid principles of good practice? (e.g. the Plan, Do, Check, Act cycle, involvement of all concerned, measurement principles)	We had several clear principles stated at the outset and everyone involved was aware of them.	We did not work on the basis of any agreed principles.

APPENDIX D

Benchmarking your HR function using the scale of effectiveness

Please refer to Figure 2.1 in Chapter 2 when completing this exercise.

Part A: Using the HR scale to benchmark your existing and future role

Items 1 to 4 below split the scale into four particular stages for you to consider when benchmarking. Look at each of them in turn and gauge your HR function against the criteria indicated. However, please think in as much depth as you can about what other indicators you might choose to demonstrate that your function has reached that particular stage.

1. Minimum but critical personnel role

Assess how well you carry out this role. Only when you are really confident that this role is being fulfilled effectively and efficiently should you attempt to develop the role of HR along this scale.

- payroll efficiency and error rate?
- health and safety – are you leaving yourself open to risk?
- recruitment efficiency and basic professionalism?
- employee relations?
- reward system, retention and staff turnover?
- absenteeism and sickness management?
- legislative requirements (e.g. contracts, other legal requirements)?

2. Effective personnel management

Consider your relationship with line managers and other internal customers. Do they call you in at the last minute for advice or are you part of their decision-making process?

For example, how soon do you hear about potential vacancies? When you do hear are you expected to just arrange advertising and interviews or do you help them to make the ultimate selection decisions?

3. Business person in personnel (HRM)

The key indicators to achieve this level are all concerned with the extent to which you are included in the detailed business plans. Do you have access to all business planning information? Would you know as much about costs, sales, customer service surveys, output figures, etc. as the operational managers themselves?

If you do have this information, have you got the necessary skills to analyse the data to enable you to hold meaningful discussions with managers and simultaneously have an input on the relevant HR issues?

4. *Total people–business integration*

For most organisations this is still an aspiration. To achieve this position HR must be regarded as a strategic business partner involved in high-level discussions about the future direction of the organisation.

The skills and knowledge required to fulfil this role include a thorough understanding of business strategy formulation, business processes and organisational structures. It also requires an ability to think long term about the HR implications of fundamental business decisions.

Part B: Changing perceptions of HR's role

While completing Part A you will have started to run up against differing, sometimes conflicting, views on what exactly the role of HR is. To address the issues this raises you need to consider the different perspectives of the various stakeholders.

What do the following want, expect or even not want from HR:

- employees?
- line managers?
- directors?
- the rest of the HR team?

How can you manage all of their expectations and ensure there is a single, coherent view of HR's role?

APPENDIX E

Which of your HR activities add the most value?

How to complete the exercise

1. Divide all your HR activity into a few broad categories and list in column 1.

2. Put a figure in column 2 to indicate their relative importance (1 = most important; 5 = least important).

3. Indicate in column 3 whether this activity is critical or not.

4. Indicate the percentage of your total time allocated to each of these activities in column 4.

5. In column 5 try to provide some indication of how this particular activity adds value and, if possible, an estimate of how much.

(1) HR activity	(2) Importance (1–5)	(3) Critical? Y/N	(4) % time	(5) How it adds value and how much (£/$)
Example: *Recruitment*	*1*	*Y*	*60*	*Speedier recruitment* *than line managers*

Now see if you are allocating the right amount of time for the highest priorities. Would there be agreement between you and line managers about what your priorities are? (Do they see a disciplinary issue today as more important than developing a good HR strategy?) Are some of your lowest value activities taking up most of your time? Should you stop doing some of these activities or delegate them to an administrator? If you are not going to be given any more resources then you must shift your existing time and effort into the areas that really make a difference.

APPENDIX F

Reviewing existing HR activities and their relative priorities

If you work in HR and you want a very simple way of trying to convert your function into a bottom line HR function then this exercise should help, but make sure you have looked at Appendix E first.

Take your list of HR activities, and those of all of your HR colleagues, and start allocating them to one of the three boxes shown in Figure F.1.

Box 1

These are all the activities that you have to carry out whether you like it or not. They do not help the organisation improve – they just keep it running smoothly. You may well have outsourced some of these already to achieve economies of scale and make some savings.

There are three main considerations in this box:

- Which of these activities are critical? I would suggest pensions administration is not as critical as making sure all forklift truck drivers have current certificates.

- Do you have systems and measures in place to ensure these activities are carried out effectively?

- Are they being carried out as efficiently as possible?

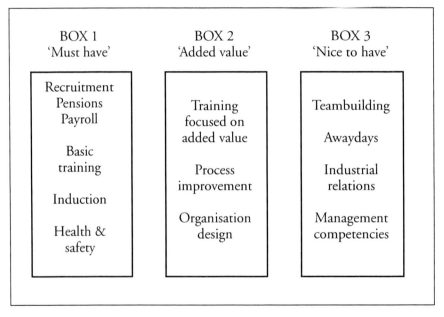

BOX 1 'Must have'	BOX 2 'Added value'	BOX 3 'Nice to have'
Recruitment Pensions Payroll Basic training Induction Health & safety	Training focused on added value Process improvement Organisation design	Teambuilding Awaydays Industrial relations Management competencies

Figure F.1 Prioritising personnel and HR activity.

Box 2

In this box the activities are designed to actually add some value (see Chapter 10) and some can be subjected to normal investment appraisal calculations such as ROI (return on investment). For example, if you help to design a new process, how much is that worth in cost savings or speedier response times? You want as much of your activity to qualify for Box 2 as possible, for obvious reasons.

Box 3

You want as few activities as possible in Box 3. They only slip into Box 3 if they are not 'must have' activities or they have no value attached. Any activities in this box should either be eliminated or shifted into Boxes 1 or 2 as soon as possible, either by making them mandatory (e.g. all managers must pass a competence assessment) or focusing them on added value (e.g. setting the teams improvement targets).

When you have finished categorising all of your work then you should estimate how much time and other resources goes into each box. This should give you a clear indication of where you are now and some of the challenges you face in becoming a bottom line HR function.

Using the HR effectiveness formula

This formula is based on the premise that the effectiveness of a methodology is inversely related to the number of assumptions on which it is based.

HR departments are often required to launch initiatives or provide solutions to achieve very unclear goals. This simple formula can be used to make sure your efforts are as effective as possible.

First, existing activity has to be categorised as follows:

- *Core activity.* All activity surrounding payroll, administration, recruitment, selection and any other normal, day-to-day activity of the HR function should be included here.

- *Added value activity.* Any activities explicitly focused on measurable improvements, in added value terms.

- *Other initiatives and non-core activity.* Any activities which do not fit into the other two categories.

The formula is normally only applicable to added value activities.

The formula is:

$$E = \frac{\frac{1}{S} \times L}{10} \times 100\%$$

Where:

E   is the overall effectiveness of the HR input (100% is maximum effectiveness).

S   is the level of sophistication used to provide a solution (on a scale of 1 = the simplest solution possible to 10 = an extremely sophisticated approach). So, a coaching initiative where specific managers are selected for their coaching ability would score 1. Training all managers in NLP (neuro linguistic programming) would score 10.

L   is the extent to which there is a direct link with the performance measures used in the business (on a scale of 0 = no link to 10 = perfect link, perfect correlation). Coaching for the sake of it scores 0; coaching to achieve business-focused targets scores 10.

APPENDIX H

Distinguishing between the cause and effect of an HR problem

Cause and effect is particularly problematic in HR. Yet understanding the difference between causes and effects is crucial if an HRM/HRD intervention is to have any chance of success.

Think about an HR problem that you are trying to deal with. Use a real example from within the group. Try to identify exactly what the 'effect' caused by the problem is. Next, look at all the possible causes of this particular problem. Which causes can you influence or impact on? Which causes are outside of HR's sphere of influence or control?

The objectives of the exercise

1.   Define the effect you are trying to resolve or improve.

2.   Use a fishbone diagram to analyse the causes of this particular effect. Highlight what you believe to be HR causes.

3.   Produce some simple suggestions as to how you would attempt to remove or lessen the impact of the causes of the effect.

Some guidelines to help you

1. Don't try to analyse any causes until you are absolutely clear what the effect is. Low morale is not necessarily an *effect*; it could equally be a cause of poor performance.

2. Also, try to indicate the size of the effect in whatever measurable way you can. If low morale is improved how much difference would it make?

3. Make sure all possible causes are included. Has the announcement about a pay freeze been the main cause? Or is it more to do with a lack of clear direction for the business? Maybe you need a new, visionary MD with excellent leadership qualities!

APPENDIX I

Standard metrics for the bottom line HR function

It has taken a whole book to give all of the reasons why I have come to the conclusion that there is no such thing as a standard set of measures or metrics in HR. However, somebody on one of my workshops, as recently as April 2000, came up to me at the end of the day and said 'so what are the measures you would recommend?'

So, for his benefit, and anyone else who has completely missed the point, here is a short list of what I would regard as a standard set of metrics for a bottom line HR function (I always do my best to give customers what they want). Of course, this list is not exhaustive.

Staff turnover and stability

Target staff turnover as a %, per annum, based on the following calculation:

$$\frac{\text{Number of leavers in 12 months}}{\text{Average number of employees over last 12 months}} \times 100\%$$

e.g. $\dfrac{15}{100} = 15\%$

Note. The best way to calculate average number of employees is to average the total employed at the end of each month. This can then form the basis for a 12-month, rolling average.

Stability should be measured in a similar way:

$$\frac{\text{Number of leavers > 12 months service}}{\text{Number of employees at end of year}} \times 100\%$$

Of course both targets should be used to manage employee retention.

Performance

Employee performance is the number one priority for the bottom line HR function. (For a much more detailed guide on how to produce employee performance measures see the author's *Measuring and Managing Employee Performance.*[1])

At the very least, all employees should be given a performance rating on a scale of 1 to 10, with 10 being excellent. Scores of 3 or less are 'unacceptable' and 8 or more means 'superior performance'. Everyone in between these goalposts is deemed to be 'acceptable'. These measures should be collected at least every six months. Then the following metrics can be collated and presented:

- % unacceptable;

- % acceptable;

- % superior;

All scores for new employees should be shown separately so that decisions can be taken about their continued employment. Of course, such metrics will be an ongoing performance indicator of the HR team's ability to select, recruit and retain the requisite level of human resource capability.

Over time there should be additional reporting on such things as number of 'unacceptables' still unacceptable after three or six months.

Similarly, aggregated figures will indicate whether the overall organisational performance is improving or not.

Organisational capability

Each job should have a list of skills, knowledge and experience requirements. Each of these headings should be assessed once a year (or more regularly for job-changers) to produce a quick *organisational capability index*.

A simple matrix can be produced to calculate this:

Job requirement	Knowledge	Skill	Experience
Product features/benefits	7	N/A	5
Sales ability	N/A	6	6
Administration	9	8	8
Total	*16*	*14*	*19*
Total out of possible (70): 49		**Percentage capability:** 70%	

All scores can be aggregated and further analysis of individual areas undertaken where necessary.

Recruitment effectiveness

The turnover, performance and capability measures will provide a great deal of information on recruitment effectiveness. Only when such information is available should two further indicators be collected:

- *efficiency* – the speed with which vacancies are filled from initial vacancy notification to offer acceptance;

- *cost* – the cost per vacancy filled

In addition, there should be a simple indicator, which shows for how long and to what extent the organisation has been working with its full complement of staff. This should be calculated every month using:

$$\frac{\text{No. employees}}{\text{Full complement no.}} \times 100\%$$

This figure should be as near to 100 per cent as possible but should be viewed in conjunction with:

$$\frac{\text{Actual salary bill}}{\text{Total complement salaries}} \times 100\%$$

Key employees

In addition to the above it is strongly recommended that any key employees/positions are identified and reported on separately. Retention and loss of key employees is a critical measure for HR.

Payback periods

It is possible to calculate payback periods for all employees. This is the time it takes before the organisation recoups its initial training and recruitment costs. The technicalities for carrying out such calculations are shown in the author's *Maximise Your ROI in Training.*[2]

Training and development

Training metrics have been notoriously difficult to collect which is why it has been treated as a specialist subject in the author's *Maximise Your ROI in Training.*[3]

Putting a £/$ sign on everything

One final comment on HR metrics – always convert measures to £££/$$$ signs wherever possible.

Notes

1. Paul Kearns (2000) *Measuring and Managing Employee Performance – A practical manual to maximise organisational performance through people.* London: Financial Times/Prentice Hall.

2. Paul Kearns (2000) *Maximise Your ROI in Training.* London: Financial Times/Prentice Hall.

3. Ibid.